James Payn

The Cupid

A Collection of Love Songs

James Payn

The Cupid
A Collection of Love Songs

ISBN/EAN: 9783337004293

Printed in Europe, USA, Canada, Australia, Japan

Cover: Foto ©Thomas Meinert / pixelio.de

More available books at **www.hansebooks.com**

THE CUPID:

A COLLECTION OF LOVE SONGS

REPRINTED FROM THE FIRST EDITION

PRIVATELY PRINTED FOR SUBSCRIBERS ONLY AT
THE MORAY PRESS
DERBY

1891

FOREWORD.

IT was intended at first that this Volume should form one of the series issued under the general title of *The Moray Library*, but a closer acquaintance with its contents convinced the Printer that it would not be suitable for the general reader; and he therefore decided, rather than withdraw it, to issue a Private Impression to Subscribers only. Of the extreme rarity of this collection of Love Poems there can be no question, but whether it was worth rescuing from oblivion is a matter of opinion. It possesses many of the faults of last century's productions, but, on the other hand, it may be considered a very fair example of a Lover's Anthology one hundred and fifty years ago. In conclusion, the Printer would remark that, had he omitted or altered any words or phrases which are not in accord with the taste of the present day, he would not have been carrying out his undertaking with the Subscribers to present them with a word for word reprint.   M.

Of this Book the following copies only have been printed, and the type broken up:—

 1 8vo on Pure Vellum, numbered 1
 3 8vo on Whatman Paper, numbered 2 to 4.
 27 8vo on Japan Vellum, numbered 5 to 31
 11 8vo on Coloured Paper, numbered 32 to 42
 14 8vo in Coloured Ink, numbered 43 to 56
 100 8vo on Van Gelder Paper, numbered 57 to 156
 288 F'cap. 8vo on Van Gelder Paper, numbered 157 to 444

Signed . for The Moray Press,

Frank Murray.

The following are the names of the Subscribers to above. Where no inconsistent addition is affixed, the title of "Esq." must be understood to follow each name.

THIS COPY was printed for the Subscriber against whose name the number thereof is written.

Ackermann, E.
Akerman, W. B.
Allen, E. G.
Allen, J.
Anderson, Bryce
Andrews, W.
Annandale, R. C.
Anonymous, per E. G. Allen
Anonymous, per R. C. Annandale
Anonymous, per John Bumpus
Anonymous, per T. B. Bumpus
Anonymous, per Combridge & Co.
Anonymous, per A. Field & Co.
Anonymous, per T. Fraser

Anonymous, per Gilbert & Field
Anonymous, per Hales & Co.
Anonymous, per C. Holt
Anonymous, per Andrew Iredale
Anonymous, per C. Mack Jost
Anonymous, per Sampson Low & Co.
Anonymous, per Elkin Mathews
Anonymous, per Melville & Co.
Anonymous, per M. E. Co.
Anonymous, per Palmer & How
Anonymous, per H. Sotheran & Co.
Anonymous, per B. F. Stevens
Anonymous, per T. Thorne
Anonymous, per H. Welter
Aylward, F. G.
Bain, Jas.
Baker, F. P.
Barnwell, H.
Barrett, Dr.
Bartlett, A. E.
Baxendine, A.
Bell, Deighton
Bethell, W.
Bigmore, E. C.
Bonser, G. G.
Bouton, J. W.
Boyd, R. J.
Brewer, A.
Briscoe, J. Potter
Brown, G. H.
Brown, W.

Bruce, R. T. Hamilton
Bryan, G.
Bumpus, John
Bumpus, T. B.
Burleigh, T.
Butler, R. F.
Caine, R. H.
Callicot, T. C.
Campbell, R.
Carlyon, T.
Caswell, C. J.
Cazenove, C. D.
Chandler, G. M.
Chichester, A. A.
Clark, W.
Claussen, W. D.
Clayton, J. P.
Clifford, Rev. W.
Cole, E. W.
Coleman, E. H.
Coleman, W. E.
Colquhoun, E. H.
Combridge, —
Coombes, G. J.
Cooper, A.
Corry, Dr.
Crisp, F. A.
Cropper, P. J.
Cruse, Henry
Davies, C.
Dawson, —
Denny, A.
Denny, F.
Dick, H. B.
Dinham, H.
Dobell, B.
Dobell, Percy
Dorey, M.
Douglas, G. N.
Downing, W.
Doxey, W
Duncan, Joseph
Duncan, Winter
Duprat, C.
Evans, C.

vi.

Evans, E. Vincent
Evans, T. H.
Falconer, C. M.
Feaks, C. E.
Fehrenbach, A.
Fenton, Rev. G. L.
Field, A.
Figgis, S.
Forfar, —
Fowle, W. F.
Francis, T.
Fraser, T.
Frederickson, C. W.
Frowd, J.
Fry, O. A.
Gauntlett, C. F.
Gerring, C.
Gibbings, W. W.
Gilbert & Field
Goodwin, D. G.
Gossett, Col.
Goulden, W. E.
Graham, M.
Graham, —
Grant, G. S.
Gray, Wm.
Groundwater, W. M.
Hales, —
Hamersley, E. G.
Harpur, T.
Hart, F. H.
Harvie-Brown, J. A.
Hatchard, —
Helme, Col.
Henley, W. E.
Hepburn, D. S.
Hilliard, F. A.
Hills, —
Hilton, W. H.
Hirst, W.
Hitchman, J.
Hockliffe, F.
Hodges & Figgis
Holme-Kay, E. A.
Holt, C.

Hopwood, O. T.
How, Jas.
Howell, Alfred
Hubbard, H. E.
Hudson, Rev. J. C.
Hullay, J. F.
Hutchinson, Thos.
Hutchinson & Co.
Hutton, W.
Hutton, W. L.
Iredale, Andrew
Jackson, R. C., F.R.H.S.
Jaggard, Wm. Jesse
James, W. H.
Johnson, A. H.
Johnston, A.
Jones, E.
Jones, John
Jones, L. W.
Kelly, W.
Kerr & Richardson
Kerslake, —
King, W.
Kinner, E.
Laing, —
Lawton, W.
Le Gallienne, R.
Lemperly, Paul
Levy, J.
Lewin, W.
Lindsay, W.
Linskill, A.
Lippincott, J. B., Co.
Little, T. W.
Lockwood, R. B.
Longbottom, —
Low, Sampson, & Co.
Lupton, J.
Lupton, A.
Lusted, C. T.
Mackey, M.
Mack Jost, C.
Macniven & Wallace
Marshall, F. E.

Mathews, Elkin
Matthews, P. L.
Matthews, S. M.
Maurais, A. H.
Maw, J.
McClurg, L.
McCormick, A. A.
McGee, J.
McLellan, —
McNab, Duncan
Melrose, A.
Melville, Mullen, & Slade
Menzies & Co., J.
Merrell, J. B.
Metcalfe, J. S.
Midland Educational Co.
Millard, G. M.
Milne, A.
Milne, R. L.
Mintern, R. E.
Mitchell, L. C.
Moffatt, A. G.
Montgomery, G.
Morgan, J. W.
Mosher, T. B.
Mücke, F. H.
Mullen, W.
Murray, A. J.
Murray, C. H.
Murray, Frank
Murray, F. E.
Murray, S. M.
Mutton, F.
Nimmo, J. C.
Nixon, W.
Noble, W.
Nottingham **Free Library**
Nutter, W., & Co.
Orr, John
Osborn, Capt.
Over, G. E.
Owen, P. G.

Palmer, G. M.
Palmer, S.
Palmer, —
Parker, —
Paul, Kegan
Pearse, P.
Perkins, Alfred
Perrett, W.
Pierce, J.
Porte, Major
Purser, E. T.
Ramsey, R.
Rand, McNally
Raltray, Jas.
Reader, A.
Redin, —
Rees, J. Rogers
Rendel, L. J.
Robson, —
Robson & Kerslake
Sampson, J.
Scott, John
Sebley, F. J.
Shaw, A.
Simmons, Thos.
Simpkin, —
Slack, J. B.
Slark, J.
Smith, A. E.
Smith, F. B.
Smith, H.
Smith, J. F.
Smith, R. E.
Smith, Thos.
Smith, William
Smith, W.
Smith, W. J.
Smithson, R. J.
Solloway, W. M. H.
Sotheran, H.
Spence, C. R.
Spurr, H.
Stanesby, S. E.
Stevens, B. F.
Stewart, Jas.

Stokoe, F. F.
Stott, Rev. Dr.
Stratton, Edward
Stuart, A.
Sutton, A.
Swann, L.
Swindells, G. H.
Taylor, A.
Taylor, E. E.
Taylor, Henry
Taylor, J.
Terry, C.
Thacker & Co.
Thistlewood, A.
Thompson, Jas.
Thorne, Thos.
Tomlinson, W.
Tutin, J. R.
Van Gorder, A. H.
Wade, W. C.
Walbrook, H. M.
Wallace, A. D. T.
Walton, —
Weadriff, G.
Weir, Harrison
Welter, H.
White, Gleeson
Whitehead, Walter
Wignell, Ernest
Williams, W. J., M.D.
Williams & Norgate
Wilson, James
Wilson, Jas.
Wilson, J.
Wilson, J. F.
Wingrove, V. H. Wyatt, M.R.C.S.
Withington, Mrs.
Yarroll, Chas.
Yeld, Rev. C.
Zaehnsdorf, J.

The reason that the number of copies exceeds the number of names in this list is that many Subscribers have taken both Large and Small Paper copies.

THE CUPID:

A COLLECTION OF LOVE SONGS,

IN TWELVE PARTS,

SUITED TO TWELVE DIFFERENT SORTS
OF LOVERS,

VIZ:—

THE FEMALE LOVER	THE TENDER LOVER
THE ADMIRING LOVER	THE WHINING LOVER
THE SLIGHTED LOVER	THE SAUCY LOVER
THE MODEST LOVER	THE MERRY LOVER
THE CONSTANT LOVER	THE PRESSING LOVER
THE JEALOUS LOVER	THE HAPPY LOVER.

Amor Omnia Vincit.

LONDON:

Printed by J. Chrichley, at Charing Cross; for
R. Dodsley, at Tully's-Head, in Pall Mall.
MDCCXXXVI.

xi.

PREFACE.

TO publish a Collection of Songs, after the World has been kindly presented with so many already, may, perhaps, seem a little needless, if not impertinent. The only excuse the Editor of these can make, is the Novelty of his Design. All the Collections which have gone before (now don't think he is going to depreciate 'em all, as is usual) are calculated, he owns, to please every-body, whilst his humble Design is only to entertain one set of People, viz., The Lovers. If the Young and the Fair are pleased, 'tis all he aims at; he does not desire the Drunkard, or the Reveler, to read his Collection; it was not design'd for his Entertainment; there are no Bacchanalias in it.

But there is one Thing which he is afraid will be urged against him as a Deficiency, and that is, that he has not mentioned the Tunes at the Head of each Song. Now, in answer to this, he humbly presumes that any thing less than printing the Tune itself is of very little Use; not to mention the extraordinary Information of letting the Reader know that the Song is to its own Tune, which is very often all they can do, their best Expedient is to tell us, that this Song is to the Tune of another Song, and that other to the Tune of this; Ianthe the Lovely, to the Tune of Ianthe the Ugly; and Ianthe the Ugly, to the Tune of Ianthe the Lovely; which gives just as much Information to the gentle Reader, as the Boy did to him that enquired his Name. My Name, says he, is my Father's. And what is thy Father's? My Father's Name is mine. And what is both your Names? They are both the same. Now he that can find out the Boy's Name or his Father's from this Information, may find out the Tune of any Song from the above-said Directions; but for such as are less cunning, 'tis presumed they are no Direction at all.

All that the Editor has to say, is, to confess that there are several Songs in this Collection not so good as he could wish, but if there are fewer bad ones in it than in any other, he shall think it has some Merit. And he further hopes, it will be of some Service to the various Kinds of Lovers, with their various Mistresses. They will here be directed to a Song upon almost any Occasion, and suited to almost any Circumstance of Temper or Humour the dear Creature may be in; and to vary a little the Words of an old Poet,—

> A Song may catch her who set Courtship flies,
> And listening, she may fall Love's Sacrifice.

INDEX.

	PAGE
As *Sylvia* in a Forrest	4
Ah! whither	10
As *Sparabella*	11
Alone by a Fountain	19
A Beauteous Face	35
Ah stay! ah turn!	43
Ah! the Shepherd's	45
Around the Plaines	46
Ah *Phillis!* why	47
Alexis shun'd	53
A gentle Warmth	60
As *Clintor*	61
At Break of Day	61
At Noon in a	62
All Thoughts of	66
Away with Sorrow	74
A Swain of Love	75
Adieu, ye pleasant	85
As when on Mountain	100
At length I feel	102
As the Snow in Vallies	106
Ah! bright *Belinda*	119
A certain Presbyterian Pair	123
Amongst the Willows	129
After the Pangs	133
As naked almost	139
A Nymph of the Plain	143

	PAGE
Amelia art thou Mad	150
As *Caelia* near	160
As *Damon* late	163
As I beneath	164
As *Cloris*, full	165
An amorous Swain	167
As *Damon* watch'd	169
As on a vernal Evening	170
Boast not, mistaken	19
Belinda's blest	28
Beneath a Beach's	44
Believe my Sighs	73
Blest as th' immortal Gods	81
By a murmuring Stream	86
Busk ye, busk ye	92
By a dismal	93
Beneath a gloomy Shade	101
Belinda's Pride's	110
Be wary, my *Caelia*	119
Bright *Cynthia's* Power	121
By the Mole on your	145
By the Toast	154
Behold I fly	159
Cruel Creature, can you	2
Clarinda, the Pride	8
Custom, alas!	22
Chloe, sure the Gods	30
Charming *Flavia*	30
Chloe when I view	32
Chloris, I cannot	36
Cecilia when with	41
Cloe be wise	44
Celia, that I once	48
Charming *Cloe*	56
Charming is your	76
Come, all ye Youths	97
Caelia, too late	123

	PAGE
Come, be free	126
Cloe's a Goddess	137
Caelia, let not Pride	144
Caelia, my dearest	144
Caelia, hoard thy	148
Come, dearest *Flavia*	155
Cloe, when I view	160
Dear *Colin* prevent	7
Damon ask'd me	22
Divine *Cecilia*	37
Dear *Cloe*, while	71
Dejected as true	72
Despairing besides	77
Did ever Swain	82
Do not ask me	125
Dorinda has such	134
Dear *Aminda*	152
Farewel, ungratful Traytor	2
From grave Lessons	5
Farewel, thou false	14
From Place to Place	17
Forgive, fair Creature	36
For many unsuccessful	60
Fair *Cloe* my Breast	69
From all uneasy	81
Fair *Iris* I love	112
Fye *Liza*, scorn	142
Genteel in Personage	13
Girls, besure	14
Give over, foolish	66
Gentle Love, this Hour	73
Go thou perpetual	93
How cruel are the Traytors	3
How hard is the Fortune	7
How wretched is	25
Hear me, ye Nymphs	45
Had I the World	88

a   xvii.

	PAGE
Help me, each	95
How wretched is	115
Hence, hence	152
Hail to the Myrtle	164
In vain poor *Damon*	12
If I love a Man	18
Is there on Earth	26
In *Chloris*	34
If from the Lustre	44
I look'd, and I sigh'd	51
It is not that I love	52
If *Corinna* would	55
I did but look	57
I cannot change	69
In vain, dear *Cloe*	70
Iris, your lovely	71
I'll range around	87
If Love's a sweet	91
I love, I doat	96
I'll tell you what	111
In *Phillis* all vile Jilts	115
I'm not one of	116
If *Phillis* denies me	121
If the Heart of a Man	130
If you sue	137
I love thee	151
Is *Hamilla*	157
I gently touch'd	166
Last Sunday at St. James's	5
Love's but the Frailty	15
Look where my dear	30
Liberia's all	38
Lost is my Quiet	69
Like a wandering	97
Lovers, who waste	108
Let us drink	122
Love is now	136

	PAGE
My Goddess, *Lydia*	31
Mistake not	50
My Days have been	52
My dear Mistress	76
My *Jeany* and I	117
My Name is honest Harry	132
May the Ambitious	158
Musing on Cares	169
Never more I will	109
No scornful Beauty	115
No more, severely	146
No, *Delia*, no	159
Oh! think not the Maid	10
Oh fie! what mean I	15
O the Lads of	20
Oh! I'll have a Husband	25
Observe the num'rous	28
O why did e'er my	50
Over the Mountains	63
Oh conceal that	74
O Love, what cruel	80
Oh! happy, happy	89
One Night, when all	99
Of all Things	104
O! I love a charming	125
Of *Anna's* Charms	135
O *Bell*, thy Looks	141
O fly from this Place	148
Oh! my Treasure	149
Pursuing Beauty	7
Phillis has such	33
Phillis, Men say	58
Prithee, *Billy*	107
Pious *Selinda*	120
Prithee, *Susan*	124
Peggy, in Devotion	127
Phillis, as her Wine	128

*a*1 xix.

	PAGE
Prithee, *Cloe* …	142
Phillis, we not grieve…	147
Poor *Damon* …	157
Phillis has a …	166
Since we, poor slavish Women	1
Strephon when you see	13
She that wou'd gain …	20
So num'rous …	31
Say cruel *Armoret* …	51
Sweet are the Charms	68
Swain, thy hopeless …	78
See what a Conquest …	91
Sad *Philocles* …	94
Since from my dear …	101
Still, *Cloe*, ply…	110
Sue to *Caelia* …	111
Silly Swain, give o'er…	114
Sylvia the Fair …	138
Since you will needs …	139
Say, lovely *Sylvia* …	153
Say, mighty Love …	167
The Groves, the Plains …	6
Tell my *Strephon* …	15
Tho' *Damon* is …	21
Too plain dear Youth …	23
'Twas when the Seas ..	24
Tho' Ladies look gay…	25
Tho' Beauty like …	29
Thou only Charmer …	31
Tell me, dear …	37
Transporting *Cloe* …	39
The Sun had just …	47
Tho', *Phyllis*, you scorn	57
The Bird that hears …	58
Tell me not …	59
Tell me, tell me …	65
The last Time I came …	67

Too lovely, cruel Fair	74
Through mournful Shades	80
Tho' cruel you seem	84
The Pain which	88
The Sun had just	101
Tho', *Flavia*	111
The Mind of a Woman	113
'Twas in this Shade	114
Three Nymphs	121
'Twas Fancy first	129
Tell me no more	133
Tho' Women	137
Tell me, *Cloe*	147
There was a Swain	153
The Lass of	156
Transported with	158
Upon *Clarinda's* panting	162
With tuneful Pipe	3
Why does my Looks	8
Whilst *Strephon*	16
What! put off	17
With Sighing and Wishing	17
When Slaves	21
When Lovers	21
Where is he gone	22
When *Fanny*, blooming	27
We all to conquering	28
With Virtues, Loves	34
When *Elismonda*	35
Without Affection	37
Who would not	39
Whilst I fondly	40
What Beauties does	40
When first *Pastora*	42
Why will *Flora*	43
Why flies *Belinda*	48
When wilt thou break	49

	PAGE
When *Delia* on the Plain	54
Were I to choose	55
When first I saw	55
Where would coy	56
What state of Life	78
Wherever I am	79
Would Fate to me	82
Why cruel Creature	83
What shall I do to	89
With broken Words	98
Whilst I gaze	99
Was *Cloe* as kind	103
Woman, thoughtless	105
Why so pale and wan	106
Why all this Whining	107
With Arts oft practis'd	108
What means this	109
When I see the bright	113
Woman's like the flutt'ring	113
Whenever, *Cloe*	127
When I court thee	130
What tho' you cannot	136
Would you have a young	140
When first I sought	145
Will you ever	148
Why should coy Beauty	150
Why should a Heart	155
When I survey	159
Whilst *Alexis*	161
When *Cloe* shines	162
Whilst on *Melanissa*	165
Ye Virgin Powers	6
Young I am	12
You meaner Beauties	32
Young *Annie's*	41
Ye Minutes	42
You I love	65

Ye Nymphs, who	84
Young *Damon*, once	86
Ye Shepherds and	90
Young *Cupid* one Day	112
Ye little *Loves*	116
Young *Corydon*	118
Yes, I could love	120
Yes, all the World	126
Ye Nymphs, no more	132
Young *Cupid* I find	134
Ye watchful Guardians	156

THE CUPID.

THE FEMALE LOVER.

SONG I.

Since we, poor slavish Women, know
Our Men we cannot pick and chuse,
To him we like, why say we no,
And both our Time and Lover lose?
With feign'd Repulses and Delays
A Lover's Appetite we pall;
And if too long the Gallant stays,
His Stomach's gone for good and all.

Or our impatient, am'rous Guest,
Unknown to us, away may steal,
And, rather than stay for a Feast,
Take up with some coarse, ready Meal.
When Opportunity is kind,
Let prudent Women be so too;
And, if the Man be to your Mind,
'Till needs you must, ne'er let him go.

The Match soon made, is happy still,
For only Love has there to do;
Let no one marry 'gainst her Will,
But stand off when her Parents wooe:
And only to their Suits be coy:
For she whom Jointure can obtain,
To let a Fop her Bed enjoy,
Is but a lawful Wench for Gain.

SONG II.

Farewel, ungrateful Traytor,
Farewel, my perjur'd Swain;
Let never injur'd Creature
Believe a Man again.
The Pleasure of possessing
Surpasses all expressing!
But 'tis too short a Blessing,
And Love too long a Pain.

'Tis easy to deceive us,
In Pity of your Pain;
But when we love, you leave us,
To rail at you in vain.
Before we have descry'd it,
There is no Bliss beside it;
But she who once has try'd it,
Will never love again.

The Passion you pretended,
Was only to obtain;
But now the Charm is ended,
The Charmer you disdain.
Your Love by ours we measure,
Till we have lost our Treasure;
But dying is a Pleasure
When living is a Pain.

SONG III.

Cruel Creature, can you leave me?
Can you then ungrateful prove?
Did you court me to deceive me,
And to slight my constant Love?

False, ungrateful, thus to wooe me,
Thus to make my Heart a Prize;
First to ruin and undo me,
Then to scorn and tyranize.

Shall I send to Heav'n my Pray'r?
Shall I all my Wrongs relate?
Shall I curse the dear Betrayer?
No, alas! it is too late.

Cupid pity my Condition;
Pierce this unrelenting Swain;
Hear a tender Maid's Petition,
And restore my Love again.

SONG IV.

How cruel are the Traytors,
Who lye and swear in jest,
To cheat unguarded Creatures,
Of Virtue, Fame, and Rest!
Whoever steals a Shilling,
Thro' Shame the Guilt conceals;
In Love the perjur'd Villain,
With Boasts the Theft reveals.

SONG V.

With tuneful Pipe, and merry Glee,
Young *Waty* won my Heart;
A blither Lad ye cou'd na see,
All Beauty without Art.
His winning Tale
Did soon prevail
To gain my fond Belief;
But soon the Swain
Gangs o'er the Plain,
And leaves me full, and leaves me full,
And leaves me full of Grief.

Tho' *Colin* courts with tuneful Song,
Yet few regard his Mane;
The Lasses a' round *Waty* throng,
While *Colin's* left alane:
In Aberdeen
Was never seen
A Lad that gave sic Pain;
He daily wooes,
And still pursues,
'Till he does all, 'till he does all,
'Till he does all obtain.

But soon as he has gain'd the Bliss,
Away then does he run;
And hardly will afford a Kiss
To silly me undone;

Bonny *Katty*,
Maggie, *Beatty*,
Avoid the roving Swain;
His wily Tongue
Be sure to shun,
Or you like me, or you like me,
Like me will be undone.

SONG VI.

As *Sylvia* in a Forrest lay
To vent her Love alone;
Her Swain *Sylvander* came that Way,
And heard her dying Moan.
"Ah! is my Love (said she) to you
"So worthless, and so vain;
"Why is your wonted Fondness now
"Converted to Disdain?

"You vow'd the Light should Darkness turn,
" E'er you'd exchange your Love;
" In Shades now may Creation mourn,
" Since you ungrateful prove.
" Was it for this I Credit gave
" To every Oath you swore?
" But ah! it seems they most deceive,
" Who most pretend t' adore.

"'Tis plain your Drift was all Deceit,
" The Practice of Mankind;
" Alas! I see it, but too late,
" My Love had made me blind.
" For you, delighted I could die;
" But oh! with Grief I'm filled,
" To think that credulous, constant I,
" Should by yourself be kill'd."

This said—all Breathless, sick and pale,
Her Head upon her Hand,
She found her Vital Spirits fail,
And Senses at a stand.
Sylvander now began to melt;
But, e'er the Word was given,
The heavy Hand of Death she felt,
And sigh'd her Soul to Heav'n.

SONG VII.

From grave Lessons and Restraint,
I'm stole out to revel here;
Yet I tremble, and I faint,
In the Middle of the Fair.
Oh! wou'd Fortune in my Way,
Throw a Lover kind and gay;
Now's the Time he soon might move
A young Heart unus'd to Love.

Shall I venture? No, no, no;
Shall I from the Danger go?
Oh! no, no, no, no, no,
I must not try, I cannot fly,
I must not, durst not, cannot fly.

Help me Nature, help me Art,
Why should I deny my Part?
If a Lover will pursue,
Like the wisest let me do;
I will fit him if he's true,
If he's false I'll fit him too.

SONG VIII.

Last Sunday at St. James's Pray'rs,
The Prince and Princess by,
I, dress'd in all my Whale-bone Airs,
Sate in a Closet nigh.
I bow'd my Knees, I held my Book,
Read all the Answers o'er;
But was perverted by a Look,
That pierc'd me from the Door.

High Thoughts of Heav'n I came to use
With the devoutest Care;
Which gay young *Strephon* made me lose,
And all the Raptures there:
He waits to hand me to my Chair,
He bows with courtly Grace,
And whispers Love into my Ear,
Too warm for that grave Place.

Love, Love, said he, by all ador'd,
My tender Heart has won;

But I grew peevish at the Word,
Desir'd he would be gone.
He went quite out of Sight, while I
A kinder Answer meant;
Nor did I for my Sins that Day
By half so much repent.

SONG IX.

The Groves, the Plains;
The Nymphs, the Swains;
The Silver Stream, and cooling Shade;
All, all declare
How false you are,
How many Hearts you have betray'd.

Dissembler go,
Too well I know
Your fatal, false, deluding Art;
To every she,
As well as me,
You make an Offering of your Heart.

SONG X.

Ye Virgin Powers defend my Heart
From am'rous Looks and Smiles,
From fancy Love, or nicer Art,
Which most our Sex beguiles.

From Sighs and Vows, and awful Fears,
That do to Pity move;
From speaking Silence, and from Tears,
Those Springs that water Love.

But if thro' Passion I grow blind,
Let Honour be my Guide;
And when frail Nature seems inclin'd,
Then place a Guard of Pride.

A Heart whose Flames are seen, tho' pure,
Needs every Virtue's Aid,
And she who thinks herself secure,
The soonest is betray'd.

SONG XI.

How hard is the Fortune of all Womankind,
For ever subjected, for ever confin'd;
The Parent controuls us until we are Wives,
The Husband enslaves the rest of our lives.

If fondly we love, yet we dare not reveal,
But secretly languish, compell'd to conceal;
Deny'd, ev'ry Freedom of Life to enjoy,
Asham'd if we're kind, and condemn'd if we're coy.

SONG XII.

Dear *Colin* prevent my warm Blushes,
Since how can I speak without Pain,
My Eyes have oft told you my Wishes,
Oh can't you their Meaning explain?
My Passion would lose by Expression,
And you too might cruelly blame;
Then don't you expect a Confession
Of what is too tender to name:

Since yours is the Province of Speaking,
Why should you expect it from me?
Our Wishes should be in our keeping,
Till you tell us what they should be:
Then quickly why don't you discover,
Did your Heart feel such Tortures as mine,
I need not tell over and over,
What I in my Bosom confine.

SONG XIII.

Pursuing Beauty, Men descry
The distant Shoar, and long to prove,
(Still richer in Variety)
The Treasures of the Land of Love.

We Women, like weak Indians stand
Inviting, from our golden Coast,
The wand'ring Rovers to our Land:
But she who trades with 'em is lost.

With humble Vows they first begin,
Stealing, unseen, into the Heart;

But by Possession settled in,
They quickly act another Part.

For Beads, and Baubles we resign,
In Ignorance our shining Store;
Discover Nature's richest Mine,
And yet the Tyrants will have more.

Be wise, be wise, and do not try,
How he can court, or you be won;
For Love is but Discovery,
When that is made, the Pleasure's done.

SONG XIV.

Why does my Looks my Thoughts betray,
And sudden Blushes in me fly?
Why do I sigh and faint away,
Since he I love would have me die?

Cou'd I but once on him prevail,
To mingle with his Joys my Smart,
That he might feel what now I ail;
But I'm too young to shew such Art.

Attractive *Cupid*, be my Care,
And look with Pity on my Pain;
Oh! break the Chains that now I wear,
Or bind *Amintor* in the same.

Haste to thy Mother, tell my Grief,
To help an harmless injur'd Maid,
That she may quickly send Relief,
And save a Heart that is betray'd.

SONG XV.

Clarinda, the Pride of the Plain,
So fam'd for her conquering Charms,
Repenting her Scorn of a Swain,
Sat pensive, and folding her Arms;
Her Lute, and her shining Attire,
Neglected, were laid at her Side:
While pining with hopeless Desire,
The Damsel thus mournfully cry'd;

Oh! cou'd the past Hours but return!
When I triumph'd in *Angelot's* Heart!
Clarinda would mutually burn,
Would mutually suffer the Smart:
But far from the Plain he is gone,
Enjoys the sweet Smiles of a Fair,
Whose Kindness the Shepherd has won,
And *Clarinda* no more is his Care.

How oft at these Feet has he lain,
Bewailing his sorrowful Fate!
But all his Complaints were in vain,
I foolishly doated on State;
I longed to be gazed on in Town,
To sparkle in golden Array,
By my Dress, and my Charms to be known,
In the Park, and at ev'ry new Play.

I thought, without Grandeur and Fame,
That Marriage no Blessing could prove;
Some wealthy young Heir was my Aim,
And I slighted poor *Angelot's* Love:
Such Madness besotted my Mind,
I receiv'd all his Sighs with Disdain;
I regarded his Vows but as Wind,
And scornfully smil'd at his Pain.

How happy my Fortune had been,
Could my Reason have conquer'd my Pride?
In Bliss I had rival'd a Queen,
Had I been my dear *Angelot's* Bride.
With him more Content I had found,
Than Grandeur and Fame can supply;
For his Fondness my Wishes had crown'd
With a Passion that never would die.

I had feasted on innocent Joy,
On the Pleasures of Kindness and Ease,
While the Fears which the Great-Ones annoy,
Had ne'er interrupted my Peace.
But ah! that glad Prospect is gone,
His Love I can never regain:
And the Loss I shall ever bemoan,
'Till Death shall relieve me from Pain.

Thus wail'd the sad Nymph all in Tears,
When the Swain to the Green did advance,

In his Hand his new Consort appears,
With a Train gaily join'd in a Dance:
Impatient, and sick at the Sight,
To the neighbouring Grove she retir'd,
(Once the Scene of her daily Delight)
And fainting, in Silence expir'd.

SONG XVI.

Oh! think not the Maid whom you scorn,
With Riches delighted can be;
Had I a great Princess been born,
My *Billy* had dear been to me:
In Grandeur and Wealth we find Woe,
In Love there is nothing but Charms,
On others your Treasures bestow,
Give *Billy* alone to these Arms.

In Title and Wealth what is lost,
In Tenderness oft is repaid:
Too much a great Fortune may cost,
Well purchas'd may be the poor Maid;
Let Gold's empty show cheat the Great,
We more real Pleasures will prove;
While they in their Palaces hate,
We in our poor Cottage will love.

SONG XVII.

Ah! whither, whither shall I fly,
A poor unhappy Maid?
To hopeless Love and Misery
By my own Heart betray'd:
Not by *Alexis* Eyes undone,
Nor by his charming faithless Tongue
Or any practis'd Art:
Such real Ills may hope a Cure,
But the sad Pains which I endure,
Proceed from fancy'd Smart.

'Twas Fancy gave *Alexis* Charms,
E'er I beheld his Face:
Kind Fancy then could fold our Arms,
And form a soft Embrace:

But since I've seen the real Swain,
And try'd to fancy him again,
I'm by my Fancy taught,
Tho' 'tis a Bliss no Tongue can tell,
To have *Alexis*, yet 'tis Hell
To have him but in Thought.

SONG XVIII.

As *Sparabella* pensive lay,
In dreary Shade along,
With woful Mood, the Love-lorn Maid
Thus wail'd in plaining Song.
The Tears forth streaming from her Eyes,
Adown her Cheeks fast flow:
Her eyes, which now no longer shine,
Her Cheeks no longer glow.

Ah! well a day! does *Colin* then
Make mock of all my Smart?
Has he so soon forgot his Vows,
Which won my Maiden Heart?
Ah Witless Damsel! why did I
So soon myself resign?
Ah why didst thou, false Shepherd, say,
Thy Heart should still be mine?

Oh! *Colin, Colin,* call to mind
What you to me did say,
As we in yonder Field were laid
Beneath the Cocking Hay;
Whilst tenderly I stroak'd thy Cheeks,
My Apron o'er thee spread,
Snatch'd hasty Kisses from thy Lips,
And lull'd thy leaning Head.

Did you not swear, that Hounds should first
With tim'rous Hares unite;
The Fox with Geese, with Lambs the Dog,
And with the Hen the Kite:
The Moon (that roves like thee) shou'd fail,
The Stars benighted prove,
The Sun (that burns like me) shou'd cease
To shine e'er thou to love?

Oh! then let wide Confusion reign,
The Hound with Hares unite;
The Fox with Geese, with Lambs the Dog,
And with the Hen the Kite:
Thou Sun, no more with Glory shine,
Ye Stars extinguish'd be;
Drop down, thou Moon, and fall to Earth,
For *Colin's* false to me.

The Damsel thus, with Eyes brim-full,
Rehears'd her piteous Woes,
When she perceiv'd her fading Life
Draw near, alas! its Close.
But first, forewarn'd by me, poor Maid!
Ah! Maid no more, she cry'd,
Ye Lasses all, shun flatt'ring Swains;
Then closed her Eyes and dy'd.

SONG XIX.

Young I am, and yet unskill'd
How to make a Lover yield:
How to keep, or how to gain;
When to love, and when to feign.
Take me, take me, some of you,
While I yet am young and true;
E'er I can my Soul disguise,
Heave my Breasts, and roll my Eyes.
Stay not till I learn the Way,
How to lie and to betray:
He that has me first is bless'd,
For I may deceive the rest.
Cou'd I find a blooming Youth,
Full of Love, and full of Truth;
Brisk and of a janty Mien,
I shou'd long to be Fifteen.

SONG XX.

In vain poor *Damon* prostrate lies,
And humbly trembles at my Feet,
While pleading Looks, and begging Sighs
With moving Eloquence entreat.
Pity persuades my trembling Breast,
That Pains so great should be redressed.

But some strange Whisper intercedes,
And tells me I must let him wait,
And makes him seal restrictive Deeds,
E'er I admit him to my State.
Women should triumph whilst they can,
Since Marriage makes 'em Slaves to Man.

SONG XXI.

Genteel in Personage,
Conduct and Equipage,
Noble by Heritage,
Generous and Free;
Brave, not romantick;
Learn'd, not pedantick;
Frolick, not frantick?
This must be he.

Honour maintaining,
Meanness disdaining,
Still entertaining,
Engaging and new:
Neat but not finical;
Sage but not cynical;
Never tyrannical,
But ever true.

SONG XXII.

Strephon when you see me fly,
Let not this your Fear create,
Maids may be as often shye
Out of Love as out of Hate:
When from you I flye away,
It is because I dare not stay.
Did I out of Hatred run,
Less you'd be my Pain and Care;
But the Youth I love, to shun,
Who can such a Trial bear?
Who, that such a Swain did see,
Who could love and flye like me?
Cruel Duty bid me go,
Gentle Love commands me stay;
Duty's still to Love a Foe,
Shall I This, or That obey!

Duty frowns and *Cupid* smiles,
That defends and this beguiles.
Ever by these Chrystal Streams
I could sit and hear thee sigh:
Ravish'd with these pleasing Dreams.
Oh! 'tis worse than Death to flye:
But the Danger is so great,
Fear gives Wings, instead of Hate.
Strephon leave me if you love me,
If you stay I am undone;
Oh! with ease you may deceive me,
Prithee charming Swain, begone:
Heav'n decrees that we should part,
That has my Vows, but you my Heart.

SONG XXIII.

Girls, besure, make Men secure,
Be never Coy in Carriage;
Put on such Grace, and taking Lure,
And when he offers Marriage,
Make no refuses
And faint Excuses,
But kindly hug the Proffer;
Let Inclination then prevail,
A seeming Slight may turn the Scale,
And she will die a Maiden stale
That ever refuses the Offer.

SONG XXIV.

Farewel, thou false *Philander*,
Since now from me you rove,
And leave me here to Wander,
No more to think of Love:
I must for ever languish,
I must for ever mourn;
From Love I now am banish'd,
And shall no more return.

Farewel, deceitful Traytor,
Farewel, thou perjur'd Swain;
Let never injur'd Creature
Believe your Vows again:

The Passion you pretended,
Was only to obtain;
For now the Charm is ended,
The Charmer you disdain.

SONG XXV.

Love's but the Frailty of the Mind,
When 'tis not with Ambition join'd;
A sickly Flame, which, if not fed, expires,
And feeding, wastes in self-consuming Fires.

'Tis not to wound a Wanton Boy,
Or Am'rous Youth, that gives the Joy;
But 'tis the Glory to have pierc'd a Swain,
For whom inferior Beauties sigh'd in vain.

Then I alone the Conquest prize,
When I insult a Rival's Eyes;
If there's Delight in Love, 'tis when I see
That Heart which others bleed for, bleed for me.

SONG XXVI.

Tell my *Strephon* that I die,
Let Echoes to each other tell,
Till the mournful Accents fly
To *Strephon's* Ear, and all is well.

But gently breath the fatal Truth,
And soften ev'ry harsher Sound;
For *Strephon* such a tender Youth,
The softest Words too deep will wound.

Now Fountains, Echoes, all be dumb,
For should I cost my Swain a Tear,
I should repent it in my Tomb,
And grieve I bought my Rest so dear.

SONG XXVII.

Oh fie! what mean I, foolish Maid,
In this remote and silent Shade,
To meet with you alone?
My Heart does with the place combine,
And both are more your Friends than mine:
Oh! I shall be undone.

A savage Beast I wou'd not fear;
Or, shou'd I meet with Villains here,
I to some Cave would run:
But such inchanting Arts you shew,
I cannot strive, I cannot go:
Oh! I shall be undone.

Ah! give those sweet Temptations o'er,
I'll touch those dang'rous Lips no more—
What, must we yet fool on?
Ah! now I yield: ah! now I fall:
And now I have no Breath at all:
And now I'm quite undone.

I'll see no more your tempting Face,
Nor meet you in this dangerous Place;
My Fame's for ever gone.
But Fame, to speak the Truth, is vain,
And every yielding Maid does gain,
By being so undone.

In such a pleasing Storm of Bliss,
To such a Bank of Paradise,
Who wou'd not swiftly run?
If you but Truth to me will swear,
We'll meet again, nor do I care
How oft I am undone.

SONG XXVIII.

Whilst *Strephon* in his Pride of Youth,
To me alone profess'd
Dissembled Passion, dress'd like Truth,
He triumph'd in my Breast.

I lodg'd him near my yielding Heart,
Deny'd him not my Arms;
Deluded by his pleasing Art,
Transported with his Charms.

The Wanderer now I lose, or share
With every lovely Maid:
Who makes the Heart of Man her Care,
Shall have her own betray'd.

Our Charms on them we vainly prove,
And think we Conquest gain;
Where one a Victim falls to Love,
A thousand Tyrants reign.

SONG XXIX.

From Place to Place, forlorn I go,
With down-cast Eyes, a silent shade;
Forbidden to declare my Woe,
To speak, till spoken to, afraid.

Me, to the Youth who caus'd my Grief,
My too consenting Looks betray;
He loves, but gives me no Relief,
Why speaks not he who may?

SONG XXX.

What! put off with one Denial?
And not make a Second Trial?
You might see my Eyes consenting,
All about me was relenting:
Women obliged to dwell in Forms,
Forgive the Youth who boldly storms.

Lovers when you sigh and languish;
When you tell us of your Anguish;
To the Nymph you'll be more pleasing,
When those Sorrows you are easing;
We love to try how far Men dare,
And never wish the Foe shou'd spare.

SONG XXXI.

With Sighing and Wishing, and Green-sickness Diet,
With nothing of Pleasure, and little of Quiet;
With Granum's Inspection, and Doctor's Direction,
But not the Specifick that suits my Complexion:
The Flower of my Age is full-blown in my Face,
Yet no Man considers my comfortless Case.

Young Women were valued, as I have been told,
In the late times of Peace, above Mountains of Gold;
But now there is fighting, we are nothing but slighting,
Few Gallants in Conjugal Matters delighting:
'Tis a shame that Mankind shou'd love killing and slaying,
And mind not supplying the Stock that's decaying.

Unlucky *Clarinda* to love in a Season,
When Mars has forgotten to do Venus Reason;
Had **I any** Hand in Rule and Command,
I'd certainly make it a Law of the Land,
That Killers of Men, to replenish the Store,
Be bound **to the** Wedlock, and made to get more.

Enacted moreover, **for** better Dispatch,
That when a good Captain meets with an o'er match;
His honest Lieutenant, with Soldier-like Grace,
Shall relieve him on Duty, and serve in his Place:
Thus Killers and Slayers of able good Men,
Without Beat **of** Drum **may** recruit 'em again.

SONG XXXII.

If I love a Man for his Money,
As many have done before,
Tho' to Night he may call me his Honey,
Tomorrow he'll call me his Whore.

Then better be **frank** and free,
And love him for loving's sake;
The sooner we Women agree,
The better's the Bargain we make.

Chuse **you a** dear Man that is **kind**,
That's generous, easy and true,
And to keep him still in the same **Mind**,
Do you keep yourself in the same **too**.

If when he begins **to change**
You fiercely the Fault reprove,
He may like others, out of Revenge,
He ne'er cou'd have lik'd **out of** Love.

To all his Follies be blind,
But mostly **to** that of roving;
When he **is** most cross, be you **most kind**,
And **teach** him to love you by loving.

If with **a** hard Word he is vex'd,
A Kiss will soon heal the Sore;
But if not one Kiss, then try the next,
And if **not** the next, the next Score.

Thus soften him by degrees,
And bring him to your Lure:
By pleasing him, yourself you may please,
And when you've half lost him, secure.

SONG XXXIII.

Boast not, mistaken Swain, thy Art
To please my partial Eyes;
The Charms that have subdu'd my Heart,
Another may despise.

Thy Face is to my Humour made,
Another it may fright:
Perhaps, by some fond Whim betray'd,
In Odness I delight.

Vain Youth, to your Confusion know,
'Tis to my Love's Excess
You all your fancied Beauties owe,
Which fade as that grows less.

For your own sake, if not for mine,
You shou'd preserve my Fire,
Since you my Swain no more will shine,
When I no more admire.

By me indeed, you are allow'd
The Wonder of your Kind:
But be not of my Judgement proud,
Whom Love has render'd blind.

SONG XXXIV.

Alone by a Fountain,
I press the cold Ground,
Lest the Rock and the Mountain
My Grief should resound.

For the Man that's so dear,
I'll never discover,
Lest the Echo should hear,
And repeat to my Lover.

The Pains that invade me
I never will tell,
Lest the World should upbraid me
With loving too well.

If my Truth cannot move,
No Fondness I'll show;
'Tis enough that I love,
And too much he should know.

SONG XXXV.

She that wou'd gain a Constant Lover,
Must at a Distance keep the Slave;
Not by a Look the Heart discover,
Men shou'd but guess the Thoughts we have.

Whilst they're in doubt, their Flame increases,
And all Attendance they will pay;
When we're possess'd, their Transport ceases,
And Vows, like Vapours, fleet away.

SONG XXXVI.

O the Lads of *Edinbro*,
They are blith and jolly;
Fine as Lairds from Top to Toe,
Free fra Melancholy.
Had I one wi me to lig,
I would be contented,
I'd nae longer care a Fig
What my Kin resented.

Willie he's a bonny Lad;
O I wish he'd Wed me!
He shou'd ken Ise nae afraid
When he gangs to bed me.
A' Night long Ise ne'er complain,
Tho' he jogd me sprightly;
But wad buckle too amain
When he meant to slight me.

Mither she a Wife has been,
Fourteen Bearns she weaned,
Time it is I shou'd begin,
Nature she sae meaned.
O some Lad of *Edinbro*,
Tak me, for I'm fading;
If you lag, the Fault's on you
That I lig a Maiden.

SONG XXXVII.

Tho' *Damon* is haughty, and seems to despise
The *Fetters* he lately has worn;
Yet he knows in his Soul, that his *Phillis's* Eyes,
Were she willing, cou'd conquer his Scorn.
Then let not Presumption so blind thee, fond *Damon*,
To think that this Humour shall e'er bring my Flame on.

If he had been humble, obliging and free,
Perhaps I had pitied his Pain;
But, since Pride and Inconstancy in him I see,
He shall know he's but lengthen'd his Chain:
For, now I perceive what the Fop does endeavour,
My Arts shall detain him my Captive for ever.

SONG XXXVIII.

When Slaves their Liberty require,
They hope no more to gain;
But you not only that desire,
But ask the Power to reign.

Think how unjust a Suit you make,
Then you will soon decline;
Your Freedom, when you please, pray take,
But trespass not on mine.

No more in vain, *Alcander*, crave,
I ne'er will grant the Thing,
That he, who once has been my Slave,
Shou'd ever be my King.

SONG XXXIX.

When Lovers for Favours petition,
Oh then they approach with Respect;
But when in our Hearts they've Admission,
They treat us with Scorn and Neglect;

'Tis dang'rous ever to try them,
So artful are Men to deceive,
'Tis safer, much safer, to fly them,
So easy are Maids to believe.

SONG XL.

Custom, alas! doth partial prove,
Nor gives us even measure:
To Maids it is a Pain to love,
But 'tis to Men a Pleasure.

They freely can their Thoughts explain,
Whilst ours must burn within:
We have got Eyes and Tongues in vain,
And Truth from us is Sin.

Men to new Joys and Conquests fly,
And yet no Hazard run.
Poor we are left if we deny;
Or if we yield undone.

Then equal Laws let Custom find,
Nor either Sex oppress:
More Freedom give to Womankind,
Or give to Mankind less.

SONG XLI.

Damon ask'd me but once, and I gave him Denial,
Intending to snap him the very next Tryal:
But, alas! he's determin'd to ask me no more,
And now make his Court to the fair *Leonore*.
But I'll have a good Heart, since I'm full well assur'd
He ne'er would have taken a Maid at her Word,
If he had been worth keeping: for this I discover,
He that takes the first Nay is a very cold Lover.
If deep were his Wound, if sincere were his Pain,
I know he'd have ask'd me again and again:
Then adieu, let him go; for why should I vex?
Since if he'd been serious, he'd allow'd for the Sex.

SONG XLII.

Where is he gone whom I adore?
The God-like Man I see no more?
Yet without Rest, his Tyrant Charms
Rent in my Breast still new Alarms.

Assist, dear Honour, take my Part,
Or I am lost with all my Art;
Tear his Idea from my Breast,
Tho' with it I am more than blest.

My Reason too, prepare your Arms,
Lest he return with greater Charms;
Love's fatal and imprison'd Dart,
Draw from my tender bleeding Heart.

SONG XLIII.

Too plain dear Youth, these tell-tale Eyes
My Heart your own declare;
But for Heav'n's sake, let it suffice,
You reign triumphant there.

Forbear your utmost Pow'r to try,
Nor further urge your Sway;
Press not for what I must deny,
For fear I shou'd obey.

But cou'd your Arts successful prove,
Wou'd you a Maid undo,
Whose greatest Failing is her Love,
And that her Love for you.

Say would you use that very Pow'r
You from her Fondness claim,
To ruin in one fatal Hour,
A Life of spotless Fame?

Ah! cease my Dear, to do an Ill
Because perhaps you may;
But rather try your utmost skill
To save me than betray.

Be you yourself my Virtu's Guard,
Defend, and not pursue,
Since 'tis a Task, for me too hard,
To strive with Love and you.

SONG XLIV.

'Twas when the Seas were roaring,
With hollow Blasts of Wind,
A Damsel lay deploring,
All on a Rock reclin'd.
Wide o'er the foaming Billows
She cast a wishful Look,
Her Head was crown'd with Willows,
That trembled o'er the Brook.

Twelve Months were gone and over,
And nine long tedious Days;
Why did'st thou, vent'rous Lover,
Why did'st thou trust the Seas!
Cease, cease then, cruel Ocean,
And let my Lover rest,
Ah! what's thy troubled Motion
To that within my Breast?

The Merchant robb'd of Treasure,
Views Tempests in Despair;
But what's the Loss of Treasure,
To losing of my Dear!
Should you some Coast be laid on,
Where Gold and Di'mond's grow,
You'd find a richer Maiden,
But none that loves you so.

How can they say that Nature
Hath nothing made in vain?
Why then beneath the Water
Doth hideous Rocks remain?
No Eyes those Rocks discover,
That lurk beneath the Deep,
To wreck the Wand'ring Lover,
And leave the Maid to Weep.

All melancholy lying
Thus wail'd she for her Dear,
Repaid each Blast with Sighing,
Each Billow with a Tear,
When o'er the wide Waves stooping,
His floating Corps she spy'd;
Then, like a Lilly drooping,
She bow'd her Head and dy'd.

SONG XLV.

Oh! I'll have a Husband, ay marry,
For why should I longer tarry,
For why should I longer tarry
Than other brisk Girls have done?
    For, if I stay,
    'Till I grow grey,
    They'll call me old Maid,
    And fusty old Jade.
So I'll no longer tarry,
But I'll have a Husband, ay marry,
If Money will buy me one.

My Mother she says I'm too coming,
And still in my Ears she is drumming,
And still in my Ears she is drumming,
That I such vain Thoughts should shun:
    My Sisters they cry,
    O fie! and oh fie!
    But yet I can see,
    They're as coming as me:
So let me have Husbands in plenty,
I'd rather have twenty times twenty,
Than die an old Maid undone.

SONG XLVI.

Tho' Ladies look gay, when of Beauty they boast,
And Misers are envy'd, when Wealth is increas'd;
The Vapours oft kill all the Joys of a Toast,
And the Miser's a Wretch, when he pays for the Feast.

The Pride of the Great, of the Rich, of the Fair,
My Pity bespeak, but Envy can't move;
My Thoughts are no farther aspiring,
No more my fond Heart is desiring,
Than Freedom, Content, and the Man that I love.

SONG XLVII.

How wretched is a Woman's Fate,
No happy Change her Fortune knows;
Subject to Man in every State,
How can she then be free from Woes?

In Youth a Father's stern Commands,
And jealous Eyes control her Will;
A Lordly Brother watchful stands
To keep her closer Captive still.

The Tyrant Husband next appears,
With awful and contracted Brow;
No more a Lover's Form he wears,
Her Slave's become her Sov'reign now.

If from this fatal Bondage free,
And not by Marriage Chains confin'd,
She, blest with single Life, can see
A Parent fond, a Brother kind.

Yet Love usurps her tender Breast,
And points a Phaenix to her Eyes;
Some darling Youth disturbs her Rest,
And painful Sighs in Secret rise.

O, cruel Powers, since you've design'd
That Man, vain Man, shou'd bear the sway,
To a Slave's Fetters add a slavish Mind,
That I may cheerfully your Will obey.

SONG XLVIII.

Is there on Earth a Pleasure
Dearer than Virtue's Fame?
In vain's the real Treasure,
When we have lost the Name.

Then let each Maid maintain it,
'Twill ask the nicest Care;
Once lost, she'll ne'er regain it,
All, all is then Despair.

THE ADMIRING LOVER.

SONG I.

When *Fanny*, blooming Fair,
First caught my ravish'd Sight,
Pleas'd with her Shape and Air,
I felt a strange Delight.
Whilst eagerly I gazed,
Admiring every Part,
And every Feature prais'd,
She stole into my Heart.

In her bewitching Eyes,
Ten thousand Loves appear;
There *Cupid* basking lies,
His Shafts are hoarded there.
Her blooming Cheeks are dy'd
With Colour all their own;
Excelling far the Pride
Of Roses newly blown.

Her well-turn'd Limbs confess
The lucky Hand of *Jove*;
Her Features all express
The beauteous Queen of Love.
What Flames my Nerves invade,
When I behold the Breast
Of that too charming Maid
Rise, suing to be prest.

Venus round Fanny's Waste,
Has her own *Cestus* bound;
There guardian *Cupids* grace,
And dance the Circle round.
How happy must he be,
Who shall her Zone unlose?
That Bliss to all but me,
May Heaven and she refuse.

SONG II.

Observe the num'rous Stars which grace
The fair expanded Skies,
So many Charms has *Lesbia's* Face,
A thousand more than Eyes.

Whene'er the beauteous Maid appears,
We cannot but admire:
But when she speaks, she charms our Ears,
And sets our Souls on Fire.

What Pity 'tis a Creature,
By Nature form'd so fair,
Divine in ev'ry Feature,
Should give Mankind Despair.

She gazes all around her,
And gains a thousand Hearts;
But *Cupid* cannot wound her,
For she has all his Darts.

SONG III.

Belinda's blest with ev'ry Grace;
See Beauty triumphs in her Face:
Her Charms such lively Rays display,
They kindle Darkness into Day.

When she appears, all Sorrow flies,
And Gladness sparkles in our Eyes;
Around her wait the flutt'ring Loves,
When graceful in the Dance she moves.

SONG IV.

We all to conquering Beauty bow,
Its pleasing Power admire;
But I ne'er knew a Face till now,
That cou'd like yours inspire.

Now I may say I met with one
Amazes all Mankind;
And like Men gazing on the Sun,
With too much Light am blind.

Soft as the tender moving Sighs,
When longing Lovers meet;
Like the divining Prophets, wise;
Like new-blown Roses, sweet:

Modest, yet gay; reserv'd, yet free;
Each happy Night a Bride:
A Mein like awful Majesty,
And yet no Spark of Pride.

The Patriarch to win a Wife,
Chaste, beautiful, and young,
Serv'd fourteen Years a painful Life,
And never thought it long.

Ah! were you to reward such Cares,
And Life so long would stay,
Not fourteen, but four hundred Years,
Would seem but as one Day.

SONG V.

Tho' Beauty like the Rose
That smiles on *Polwarth* Green
In various Colours shows,
As 'tis by the Fancy seen:
Yet all its different Glories lie
United in thy Face;
And Virtue, like the Sun on high,
Gives Rays to every Grace.

So charming is her Air,
So smooth, so calm her Mind,
That to some Angel's Care
Each Motion seems assign'd:
But yet so chearful, sprightly, gay,
The joyful Moments fly,
As if for Wings they stole the Ray,
She darteth from her Eye.

Kind Amrous *Cupids*, while
With tuneful Voice she sings
Perfume her Breath, and smile,
And wave their balmy Wings:
But as the tender Blushes rise,
Soft Innocence doth Warm,
The Soul in blissful Extasies
Dissolveth in the Charm.

SONG VI.

Look where my dear *Hamilla* smiles,
Hamilla heavenly Charmer,
See how with all their Arts and Wiles,
The Loves and Graces arm her.
A Blush dwells glowing on her Cheeks,
Fair Seats of youthful Pleasures;
There Love in smiling Language speaks,
There spread his rosy Treasures.

O fairest Maid, I own thy Power,
I gaze, I sigh, I languish;
Yet ever, ever will adore,
And triumph in my Anguish.
But ease, oh Charmer! ease my Care,
And let my Torments move thee;
As thou art fairest of the Fair,
So I the dearest love thee.

SONG VII.

Chloe, sure the Gods above
For our Joys did you compose,
Graceful as the Queen of Love,
Wanton as the billing Dove,
Fragrant as the blowing Rose.

Wit and Beauty both we find
Striving which will arm you most:
Doubly, *Chloe*, thus you bind,
Had not Nature made you kind,
We, alas! were doubly lost.

SONG VIII.

Charming *Flavia*, cast your Eyes
On the Slave that's at your Feet,
See he panting, trembling lies,
And dare not rise till you think fit.

But rather, *Flavia*, let him lie;
When he, ambitious Slave, is dead,
Kings will his happy state envy,
And wish they in his Place had laid.

Then since to die at *Flavia's* Feet,
Can thus from Monarchs Envy move;
How blest the Youth! whom she doth meet,
In all the Extasies of Love!

Oh were the mighty Bliss but mine,
Immortal *Jove* would envy me;
'Midst heavenly Joys he would repine,
And own me far more blest than he.

SONG IX.

Thou only Charmer I admire,
My Heart's Delight, my Soul's **Desire**,
Possessing thee I've greater Store,
Than were I Lord of Indian's Shore.

Were every other Woman free,
And in the World no Man but me,
I'd single thee from all the rest,
To sweeten Life and make me blest.

SONG X.

So num'rous *Flavia's* Charms appear,
As may her Form display
In all the Dresses of the Year,
And Beauties of the Day.

Calm and serene, like *Spring* her Air;
Like *Autumn* soft her Mold;
Her Face, like *Summer*, blooming fair;
Her Heart like *Winter*, Cold.

Her Bosom, Cynthia's full-orb'd Light;
Her Cheeks, *Noon's* Rays adorn;
Her Tresses shew the falling *Night;*
Her Eyes, the rising *Morn.*

SONG XI.

My Goddess, *Lydia*, heavenly fair,
As Lilly sweet, as soft as Air,
Let loose thy Tresses, spread thy Charms,
And to my Love give fresh Alarms.

O! let me gaze on those bright Eyes,
Tho' sacred Lightning from them flies,
Shew me that soft, that modest Grace,
Which paints with charming Red thy Face.

Give me *Ambrosia* in a Kiss,
That I may rival *Jove* in Bliss;
That I may mix my Soul with thine,
And make the Pleasures all divine.

O hide thy Bosom's killing White,
(The Milky Way is not so bright)
Lest you my ravish'd Soul oppress
With Beauty's Pomp and sweet Excess.

SONG XII.

Chloe when I view thee smiling,
Joys celestial round me move,
Pleasing Visions Care beguiling,
Guard my State and crown my Love.

To behold thee gaily shining,
Is a Pleasure past designing,
Every Feature charms my Sight.
But, oh Heav'ns! when I'm caressing,
Thrilling Raptures never ceasing,
Fill my Soul with soft Delight.

Oh! thou lovely dearest Creature!
Sweet Enslaver of my Heart;
Beauteous Master-piece of Nature,
Cause of all my Joy and Smart!

In thy Arms enfolded lay me,
To dissolving Bliss convey me,
Softly sooth my Soul to rest;
Gently, kindly, oh my Treasure!
Bless me, let me die with Pleasure,
On thy panting snowy Breast.

SONG XIII.

You meaner Beauties of the Night,
Who poorly satisfy our Eyes,
More with your Number than your Light,
Like common People of the Skies,
What are you when the Moon doth rise?

You Violets that first appear,
By your fine purple Mantles known,
Like the proud Virgins of the Year,
As if the Spring were all your own;
What are you when the Rose is blown?

You warbling Chanters of the Wood,
Who fill our Ears with Nature's Lays,
Thinking your Passion's understood
By meaner Accents; What's your Praise
When *Philomel* her Voice doth raise?

You glorious Trifles of the East,
Whose Estimations Fancies raise,
Pearls, Rubies, Sapphires, and the rest
Of glittering Gems; What is your Praise,
When the bright Di'mond shews his Rays?

So when my Princess shall be seen
In Beauty of her Face and Mind,
By Virtue first, then Choice, a Queen;
Tell me if she were not design'd
T' eclipse the Glory of her kind?

The Rose, the Violet, the whole Spring,
Unto her Breath for Sweetness run,
The Di'mond darkened in the Ring,
If she appear the Moon's undone,
As in the presence of the Sun.

SONG XIV.

Phillis has such charming Graces,
Beauty triumphs in her Eye;
She was made for the Embraces
Of some mighty Deity.
Phillis has such charming Graces,
I must love her though I die.

Have a Care, celestial Creature,
Coyness may your Beauty pall;
You an Angel are by Nature;
Angels by their Pride lost all.
Have a Care, celestial Creature,
Lest I triumph in your Fall.

SONG XV.

In *Chloris* all soft Charms agree,
Inchanting Humour, pow'rful Wit ;
Beauty from Affectation free,
And for eternal Empire fit.
Where'er she goes, Love waits her Eyes,
The Women envy, Men adore ;
But did she less the Triumph prize,
She wou'd deserve the Conquest more.

The Pomp of Love so much prevails,
She begs, what none else wou'd deny her ;
Makes such advances with her Eyes,
The Hopes she gives prevents Desire ;
Catches at every trifling Heart,
Seems warm with ev'ry glimmering Flame,
The common Prey so deads the Dart,
It scarce can pierce a noble Game.

I cou'd lie Ages at her Feet,
Adore her, careless of my Pain,
With tender Vows her Rigours meet,
Depair, love on, and not complain,
My Passion from all Change secure.
No Favours raise, no Frown controls,
I any Torment can endure,
But hoping with a Crowd of Fools.

SONG XVI.

With Virtues, Loves, and Graces join'd
Not *Eve* in *Eden* ere she sinned,
Clarissa various Charms out-shined,
And raised more Admiration.
Her Stature, Shape, her Mein and Air,
Her Bosom, Breasts, her Neck and Hair,
Her Eyes so bright, and Face so fair,
Are fraughted with Temptation.

Ye Sages, say by Flesh and Blood
How can such Beauties be withstood?
What Hermit wou'd not, if he cou'd,
To Wantonness persuade her?

But round her stock of Innocence,
The flaming Swords of Wit and Sense,
Turn every Way, in her Defence,
Against the bold Invader.

O fairest of the fairest kind,
Thou perfect Person, purest Mind,
Behold an amorous Swain resigned
Entire to your Devotion.
My Passion's bound thy Virtue's Slave!
No lawless Boon I'll dare to crave,
Nor indiscreetly misbehave,
Tho' all my Soul's in Motion.

Yet whilst I melt in tender Sighs,
O let soft Pity meet my Eyes,
And gently treat the Sacrifice
Your Charms have made so willing.
While due Decorum I maintain,
O kindly use your love-sick Swain;
Sustain my Hopes, however vain,
For Frowns from you were killing.

When thus in sacred Friendship blest,
Each shall create in th' other's Breast
A Pleasure not to be exprest,
Nor felt by foolish Rovers.
How gently then will Life decay,
And Time unheeded steal away,
In Conversation good and gay,
Becoming virtuous Lovers?

SONG XVII.

A Beauteous Face, fine Shape, engaging Air,
With all the Graces that adorn the Fair,
If these cou'd fail their so accustomed Parts,
And not secure the Conquest of our Hearts,
Sylvia has yet a vast reserve in store,
At Sight we love, but Hearing must adore.

There falls continued Musick from her Tongue,
The Wit of *Sappho* with her artful Song;
From Syrens thus we lose the power to fly,
We listen from the Charm and stay to die.
Ah! lovely Nymph, I yield, I am undone,
Your Voice has finished what your Eyes begun.

SONG XVIII.

Forgive, fair Creature, form'd to please,
Forgive a wond'ring Youth's Desire:
Those Charms, those Virtues, when he sees,
How can he see and not admire?

While each the other still improves,
The fairest Face, the fairest Mind;
Not, with the Proverb, he that loves,
But he that loves you not is blind.

SONG XIX.

When *Elismonda* shews her Face,
The killing Air, the melting Grace,
A thousand Lovers round her fly,
A thousand on her Beauties die.

In her smooth Cheeks are gaily spread
The Lilly's White, the Rose's Red,
But never Odours of the Spring,
Such Incense as her Breath could bring.

What Raptures does her Voice dispense!
How soft the Sounds, how strong the Sense!
The Sweetness reconciles the Smart,
And while it conquers, mends the Heart.

When other Dangers bend the Bow,
We fly the Field, or fight the Foe;
But here a different turn is found,
We court the Dart and kiss the Wound.

SONG XX.

Chloris, I cannot say your Eyes
Did my unwary Heart surprize;
Nor will I swear it was your Face,
Your Shape, or any nameless Grace;
For you are so entirely fair,
To love a Part Injustice were.

No drowning Man can know which Drop
Of Water his last Breath did stop:

So when the Stars in Heav'n appear,
And join to make the Night look clear,
The Light we no one's Bounty call,
But the united Work of all.

He that doth Lips or Hands adore,
Deserves them only, and no more;
But I love all, and every Part,
And nothing else can ease my Heart:
Cupid that Lover weakly strikes,
Who can express what 'tis he likes.

SONG XXI.

Without Affectation, gay, youthful and pretty;
Without Pride or Meanness, familiar and witty;
Without Form, obliging, good natured and free;
Without Art, as lovely as lovely can be.

She acts what she thinks, and thinks what she says,
Regardless alike both of Censure and Praise;
But her Thoughts and her Words and her Actions are such,
That none can admire them, or praise them too much.

SONG XXII.

Tell me, dear Charmer, tell me why
All other Joys so quickly cloy,
All but the Joys of loving thee,
And they alone immortal be?
They neither dull the Mind nor Sense,
Nor lose their pleasing Influence.

For ever I, with fierce Desire,
Cou'd gaze on thee, and never tire;
My ravished Ears cou'd all Day long
Feast on the Musick of thy Tongue;
And when that fails, yet still in you
I something find that's ever new.

SONG XXIII.

Divine *Cecilia*, now grown old,
Must yield to one of fresher Mold:
Her Strains brought Angels down to hear,
And listen with a ravished Ear.

But here such Harmony of Shape
Might tempt them to another Rape;
And make them leave their Heav'n behind,
To wed the Daughters of Mankind.

There needs no Angel from the Skies,
A real Goddess charms our Eyes;
As Venus to Æneas prov'd,
So look'd, so talk'd, so smil'd, so mov'd.

When *Purcel's* melting Notes she sings,
Applauding *Cupids* clap their Wings,
Mistake her for their Cyprian Dame,
Her Infant too for one of them.

She graceful leads the dancing Choir,
As smooth as Air, as quick as Fire;
Now rising like the bounding Roe,
Now sinks as Flakes of feather'd Snow.

In Sacred Story may be read,
How Dancing cost *St. John* his Head;
We here expose a nobler Part,
For sure no Head is worth a Heart.

SONG XXIV.

Liberia's all my Thought and Dream,
She's all my Pleasure and my Pain;
Liberia's all that I esteem,
And all I fear is her Disdain.

Her Wit, her Humour, and her Face,
Please beyond all I felt before;
Oh! why can't I admire her less?
Or, dear *Liberia* love me more.

Like Stars, all other female Charms
Ne'er touch my Heart, but feast mine Eye;
For she's the only Sun that warms,
With her alone I'd live and die.

Immortal Pow'rs, whose Work divine
Inspires my Soul with so much Love,
Grant your *Liberia* may be mine,
And then I share your Joys above.

SONG XXV.

Who would not gaze away his heart
On *Mariana's* Eyes,
Did not her high and just Disdain
The bold Delight chastise?

Mirth and Joy she spreads around,
Like the Sun's chearful Light,
When his returning Beams destroy
The Empire of the Night.

Her Beauty with Amazement strikes
(If with no more) the old;
Her Virtue tempers with Despair
The Youthful and the Bold.

Her Goodness so disarms her Wit
Of the offensive Part;
Whilst others only charm the Ear,
She steals the very Heart.

Let us no more defame the Fair,
But learn to praise again;
Bright *Mariana's* Worth demands
A new and nobler Strain.

So to the feathered Kind the Spring
Restores their wonted Voice;
On every Bough they sit and sing,
And court their new-made Choice.

SONG XXVI.

Transporting *Cloe*, lovely, fair,
How beauteous do thy Charms appear,
When smiling Graces from thee spring!
A thousand *Cupids* in thy Eyes,
To touch the Heart with sweet Surprize,
Their Bows with Vigour string.

Goddess of immortal Pleasure,
In thy Arms is Beauty's Treasure:
Charming Rays around thee shine,
Roses in thy Cheeks are blowing,
Music from thy Accents flowing;
Love creates thee all divine.

SONG XXVII.

Whilst I fondly view the Charmer,
Thus the God of Love I sue;
Gentle *Cupid*, pray disarm her,
Cupid if you love me, do.
Of a thousand smiles bereave her,
Rob her Neck, her Lips, her Eyes;
The remainder still will leave her
Power enough to tyrannize.

Shape and Feature, Flame and Passion,
Still in every Breast will move;
More is supererogation,
Mere Idolatry of Love:
You may dress a World of *Cloes*,
In the Beauty she can spare:
Hear him *Cupid*, who no Foe is
To your Altars, or the Fair.

SONG XXVIII.

What Beauties does *Flora* disclose?
How sweet are her Smiles upon *Tweed?*
Yet *Moggy's* still sweeter than those,
Both Nature and Fancy exceed:
Nor *Daisy*, nor sweet blushing *Rose*,
Nor all the gay Flow'rs of the Field,
Nor *Tweed* gliding gently through those,
Such Beauty and Pleasure does yield.

The Warblers are heard in the Grove,
The Linnet, the Lark, and the Thrush;
The Black-bird, and sweet cooing Dove,
With Music enchant every Bush.
Come let us go forth to the Mead,
Let us see how the Primroses spring;
We'll lodge in some Village on *Tweed*,
And love while the feathered Folk sing.

How does my Love pass the long Day,
Does *Moggy* not tend a few Sheep?
Do they never carelessly stray,
While happily she lies asleep?

Tweed's Murmurs should lull her to rest,
Kind Nature indulging my Bliss,
To relieve the soft Pains of my Breast,
I'd steal an Ambrosial Kiss.

'Tis she does the Virgins excel,
No Beauty with her may compare;
Love's Graces all round her do dwell;
She's fairest, where thousands are fair.
Say, Charmer, where do thy Flocks stray?
O! tell me at Noon where they feed?
Shall I seek them on sweet winding *Tay*,
Or the pleasanter Banks of the *Tweed?*

SONG XXIX.

Cecilia when with artful Note
You charm th' attentive Ear;
And warble from your tuneful Throat
What Seraphims might hear,

My Soul in Raptures feels the Song,
And dwells upon the Sound:
So *Syrens* draw the list'ning Throng,
And please them while they wound.

SONG XXX.

Young *Annie's* budding Graces claim
Th' inspir'd Thought, and softest Lays,
And kindle in the Breast a Flame,
Which must be vented in her praise.
Tell us ye gentle Shepherds, have you seen,
E'er one so like an Angel tread the Green.

Ye Youth be watchful of your Hearts,
When she appears, take the Alarm;
Love on her Beauty points his Darts,
And wings an Arrow on each Charm:
Around her Eyes and Smiles the Graces sport,
And to her snowy Neck and Breast resort.

But vain must ev'ry Caution prove,
When such enchanting Sweetness shines;
The wounded Swain must yield to Love,
And wonder, though he hopeless pines.
Such Flames the foppish Butterfly should shun,
The Eagle's only fit to view the Sun.

She as the opening Lilly fair,
Her lovely Features are compleat:
Whilst Heav'n, indulgent, makes her share
With Angels, all that's Wise and Sweet.
These Virtues, which divinely deck her Mind,
Exalt each Beauty of th' inferior kind.

Whether she love the rural Scenes,
Or sparkles in the airy Town,
O happy he! her Favour gains;
Unhappy, if she on him frown.
The Muse unwilling, quits the lovely Theme,
Adieu, she sings, and thrice repeats her Name.

SONG XXXI.

Ye Minutes bring the happy Hour
And *Cloe* blushing to the Bow'r;
Then shall all idle Flames be o'er,
Nor Eyes, or Heart, e'er wander more:
Both, *Cloe*, fixed for e'er on thee,
For thou art all thy Sex to me.

A Guilty is a false Embrace,
Corinna's Love's a fairy chase:
Begone thou Meteor, fleeting Fire,
And all that can't survive Desire:
Cloe my Reason moves, and Awe,
And *Cupid* shot me when he saw.

SONG XXXII.

When first *Pastora* came to Town,
The fresh Desires of every Heart,
Her Innocence so fenc'd her own,
She laughed at *Cupid* and his Dart,

Her Looks might all the World enflame,
Themselves, yet cold as freezing Snow:
Which the bold Hand that thinks to tame,
Soon with the unusual Heat will glow.

As when a Comet does appear,
We Stars and Moon no more respect,
So while *Pastora* guides our Sphere,
All former Beauties we neglect.

THE SLIGHTED LOVER.

SONG I.

Why will *Flora*, when I gaze,
My ravished Eyes reprove?
And hide 'em from the only Face
They can behold with Love?

To shun her Scorn, and ease my Care,
I seek a Nymph more kind;
And while I rove from fair to fair,
Still gentle Usage find.

But oh! how faint is every Joy,
Where Nature has no Part?
New Beauties may my Eyes employ,
But you engage my Heart.
So restless Exiles, doomed to roam,
Meet Pity ev'ry where;
Yet languish for their native Home,
Tho' Death attends them there.

SONG II.

Ah stay! ah turn! ah! whither would you flie,
Too charming, too relentless Maid!
I follow not to conquer, but to die;
You of the fearful are afraid.

In vain I call; for she like fleeting Air,
When prest by some tempestuos Wind,
Flies swifter from the Noise of my Despair,
Nor casts one pitying Look behind.

SONG III.

If from the Lustre of the Sun,
To catch your fleeting Shade you run,
In vain is all your Haste, Sir;
But if your Feet reverse the Race,
The Fugitive will urge the Chace,
And follow you as fast, Sir.

Thus, if at any Time as now,
Some scornful *Cloe* you pursue,
In Hopes to overtake her;
Be sure you ne'er too eager be,
But look upon 't—as cold as she,
And seemingly forsake her.

So I and *Laura* t' other Day,
Were coursing round a Cock of Hay,
While I could ne'er o'er get her.
But when I found I ran in vain,
Quite tir'd, I turn'd back again,
And, flying from her met her.

SONG IV.

Beneath a Beach's grateful Shade,
Young *Colin* lay complaining;
He sigh'd, and seem'd to love a Maid,
Without Hopes of obtaining.

For thus the Swain indulged his Grief,—
Tho' Pity cannot move thee,
Tho' thy hard Heart gives no Relief,
Yet *Peggy*, I must love thee.

SONG V.

CLOE be wise, no more perplex me,
Slight not my Love at such a rate;
Should I your Scorn return, 'twill vex you,
Love much abused will turn to Hate.

How can so lovely fair a Creature,
Put on the looks of cold Disdain?
Women were first design'd by Nature,
To give a Pleasure, not a Pain.

Kindness creates a Flame that's lasting,
When other Charms are fled away;
Think then the Time you now are wasting,
Throw off those Frowns and Love obey.

SONG VI.

Ah! the Shepherd's mournful Fate,
When doom'd to love, and doom'd to languish;
To bear the scornful Fair One's Hate,
Nor dare disclose his Anguish.

Yet eager Looks, and dying Sighs,
My secret Soul discover,
While Rapture trembling thro' my Eyes,
Reveal how much I love her.

The tender Glance, the red'ning Cheek,
O'erspread with rising Blushes,
A thousand various Ways they speak,
A thousand various Wishes.

For oh! that Form so heavenly fair,
Those languid Eyes so sweetly smiling,
That artless Blush, and modest Air,
So fatally beguiling.

Thy every Look, and every Grace,
So charm whene'er I view thee;
Till Death o'ertake me in the Chace,
Still will my Hopes pursue thee.

Then when thy tedious Hours are past,
Be this last Blessing given,
Low at thy Feet to breath my last,
And die in sight of Heaven.

SONG VII.

Hear me, ye Nymphs, and every Swain,
I'll tell how *Peggy* grieves me,
Tho' thus I languish, thus complain,
Alas! she ne'er believes me.
My Vows and Sighs, like silent Air,
Unheeded never move her;
At the bonny Bush aboon *Traquair*,
'Twas there I first did love her;

That Day she smil'd, and made me glad,
No Maid seem'd ever kinder;
I thought myself the luckiest Lad,
So sweetly there to find her.
I tried to sooth my amorous Flame
In Words that I thought tender;
If more there past I'm not to blame,
I meant not to offend her.

Yet now she scornful flies the Plain,
The Fields we then frequented;
If e'er we meet, she shows Disdain,
And looks as ne'er acquainted.
The bonny Bush bloom'd fair in *May*,
Its Sweets I'll ay remember;
But now her Frowns make it decay,
It fades as in *December*.

Ye rural Powers, who hear my Strains,
Why thus should *Peggy* grieve me?
Oh! make her Partner in my Pains,
Then let her Smiles relieve me,
If not my Love will turn Despair,
My Passion no more tender;
I'll leave the Bush aboon *Traquair*,
To lonely Wilds I'll wander.

SONG VIII.

Around the Plaines my Heart has rov'd,
The Brown, the Fair my Flames approv'd.
The Pert, the Proud, by turns have loved,
And kindly filled my Arms.

I danc'd, I sung, I talk'd, I toy'd,
While this I woo'd, I that enjoy'd,
And e'er the Kind with Kindness cloy'd,
The Coy resigned her Charms.

But now, alas! those Days are done,
The Wrong'd are all reveng'd by one,
Who like a frighted Bird is flown,
Yet leaves her Image here.

O could I yet, her Heart recal,
Before her Feet my Pride would fall,
And for her Sake, forsaking all,
Wou'd fix for ever there.

SONG IX.

Ah *Phillis!* why are you less *tender*
To my despairing *Amore?*
Your Heart you have promised to *tendre,*
Do not deny the *Retour.*
My Passion I cannot *defendre,*
No, no, Torments increase *tous les Jours.*

To forget your kind Slave is *Cruelle,*
Can you expect my *Devoir!*
Since *Phillis* is grown *infidelle,*
And wounds me at ev'ry *Revoir!*
Those Eyes which were once *Agreeable,*
Now, now, are Fountains of Black *Desospire.*

Adieu to my false *Esperance,*
Adieu *les Plaisirs des beaux Jours;*
My *Phillis* appears at *Distance,*
And slights my unfeigned *Efforts:*
To return to her Vows *impossible;*
No, no, adieu to the Cheats of *Amours.*

SONG X.

The Sun had just withdrawn his Fires,
And *Phoebe* shone with milder Ray,
When *Thyrsis* to the Grove retires,
As Love had pointed out the Way.

His trembling Knees the Turf receives,
His aching Head the Cowslips press;
His Breast, that Sighs alone had eased,
At last gave way to this Address:

O Queen, that guid'st the silent Hours,
If e'er *Endymion* sooth'd thy Pain,
By all thy Joys in *Carian* Bow'rs,
Restore me *Rosalind* again.

To thee my mournful Plaint I send,
Protectress of the virtuous Mind,
Do thou thy chaste Assistance lend,
Venus is leud, and *Cupid* blind.

Behold these Cheeks, how pale, how wan!
That once were graced with rosie Pride:
Dim are my Eyes, their Lustre gone,
My Lips a purple Hue deride.

To wretched me it nought avails,
That *Phoebus* self has strung my Lyre;
Since *Plutus*, worthless God, prevails,
And only sordid Wealth can fire.

The Nightingale that pines with Love,
With melting Notes does Grief suspend;
Me Verse, nor sweetest Sounds can move,
My Torment she alone can end.

But hark the Raven's direful Croak,
Joined with the Owl's ill-boding Shriek,
In frightful consort Fate have spoke;
Alas! my Love-sick Heart will break.

Too cruel Nymph, haste, haste away,
And see your Victim prostrate lye;
I faint, I can no longer stay,
O *Rosalind*, for thee I die!

SONG XI.

Celia, that I once was blest
Is now the Torment of my Breast;
Since to cure me, you bereave me
Of the Pleasure I possest:
Cruel Creature to deceive me,
First to love, and then to leave me.

Had you the Bliss refus'd to grant,
I then had never known the want;
But possessing once the Blessing,
Is the Cause of my Complaint.
Once possessing is but tasting,
'Tis no Bliss that is not lasting.

Celia now is mine no more,
But I am her's and must adore;
Not to leave her will endeavour;
Charms, that captiv'd me before,
No Unkindness can dissever;
Love that's true is Love for ever.

SONG XII.

Why flies *Belinda* from my Arms!
Or shuns my kind Embrace?
Why does she hide her blooming Charms?
And when I come forsake the Place.

Like some poor Fawn, whom every Breath
Of Air does so surprize;
In the least Wind he fancies Death,
And pants at each approaching Noise.

Leave, leave thy Mother's Arms for Shame!
Nor fondly hang about her;
Thou'rt now of Age to play the Game,
And ease a Lover's Pain without her.

SONG XIII.

When wilt thou break, my stubborn Heart?
O Death, how slow to take my Part!
Whatever I pursue, denies,
Death, Death itself like *Myra* flies.

Love and Despair, like Twins, possest
At the same fatal Birth my Breast;
No Hope could be, her Scorn was all
That to my destin'd Lot cou'd fall.

I thought, alas! that Love cou'd dwell
But in warm Climes, where no Snow fell;
Like Plants that kindly Heat require,
To be maintained by constant Fire.

That without Hope, 'twou'd die as soon,
A little Hope——But I have none:
On Air the poor Camelions thrive;
Deny'd even that, my Love can live.

As toughest Trees in Storms are bred,
And grow, in spite of Winds, and spread;
The more the Tempest tears and shakes
My Love, the deeper Root it takes.

Despair, that Aconite does prove,
And certain Death to others Love,
That Poison, never yet withstood,
Does nourish mine and turn to Food.

O! for what Crime is my torn Heart
Condemn'd to suffer deathless Smart?
Like sad *Prometheus*, thus to lie
In endless Pain, and never die.

THE MODEST LOVER.

SONG I.

Mistake not, *Celia*, the Design,
When I your Worth proclaim;
Or dedicate a Verse of mine,
To your distinguish'd Name.
The Muses were ordain'd to shew
The Glories of your Sex;
Then why should what is sung of you,
Your modest Mind perplex?

At Thoughts of you, my Muse takes Wing,
My tender Bosom warms:
Indulge me then with leave to sing,
Or lay aside your Charms.
No grateful Answer I desire,
No Favours I implore;
'Tis all I want, or will require,
Allow me to adore.

SONG II.

O why did e'er my Thoughts aspire
To wish for that no Crown can buy?
'Tis Sacrilege, but to desire
What she in Honour will deny.

As *Indians* do the Easter Skies,
I at a Distance must adore
The brighter Glories of her Eyes,
And never dare pretend to more.

SONG III.

I look'd, and I sigh'd, and I wish'd I cou'd speak,
For I very fain wou'd have been at her;
But when I strove most my Passion to break,
Still then I said least of the Matter.
I swore to myself, and resolv'd I wou'd try
Some Way my poor Heart to recover;
But that was all vain, for I sooner could die
Than live with forbearing to love her.

Dear *Celia* be kind then; and since your own Eyes
By Looks can command Adoration,
Give mine leave to talk too, and do not despise
Those Oglings that tell you my Passion.
We'll look and we'll love, and tho' neither shou'd speak,
The Pleasure we'll still be pursuing;
And so without Words, I don't doubt we may make
A very good end of this Wooing.

SONG IV.

Say cruel *Armoret*, how long
In Billet-doux, and humble Song,
Shall poor *Alexis* woo?
If neither writing, sighing, dying,
Reduce you to a soft complying,
O! when will you come to?

Full thirteen Moons are now pass'd o'er,
Since first those Stars I did adore,
That set my Heart on Fire:
The conscious Play-house, Parks, and Court,
Have seen my Sufferings made you Sport,
Yet was I ne'er the nigher.

A faithful Lover shou'd deserve
A better Fate than thus to starve,
In sight of such a Feast.
But oh! if you'd not think it fit
Your hungry Slave shou'd taste one bit,
Give some kind Looks at least.

SONG V.

My Days have been so wondrous free,
The little Birds that fly,
With careless Ease, from Tree to Tree,
Were but as blest as I.

Ask gliding Waters, if a Tear
Of mine increas'd their Stream;
Or ask the flying Gales, if e'er
I lent a Sigh to them.

But now my former Days retire,
And I'm by Beauty caught;
The tender Chains of sweet Desire,
Are fixt upon my Thought;

An eager Hope within my Breast,
Does every Doubt controul;
And lovely *Nancy* stands confest,
The Fav'rite of my Soul.

Ye Nightingales, ye twisting Pines,
Ye Swains that haunt the Grove,
Ye gentle Echo's, breezy Winds,
Ye close Retreats of Love;

With all of Nature, all of Art,
Assist the dear Design;
O teach a young unpractis'd Heart,
To make her ever mine.

The very Thought of Change I hate,
As much as of Despair;
And hardly covet to be great,
Unless it be for her.

'Tis true, the Passion in my Mind
Is mixt with soft Distress;
But while the Fair I love is kind,
I cannot wish it less.

SONG VI.

It is not that I love you less
Than when before your Feet I lay,
But to prevent the sad Encrease
Of hopeless Love, I keep away.

In vain (alas), for every Thing,
Which I have known belong to you,
Your Form does to my Fancy bring,
And makes my old Wounds bleed anew.

Who in the Spring from the new Sun,
Already has a Feaver got,
Too late begins those Shafts to shun,
Which *Phaebus* through his Veins has shot.

Too late he would the Pain assuage,
And to thick Shadows does retire;
About with him he bears the Rage,
And in his tainted Blood the Fire.

But vow'd I have, and never must
Your banish'd Servant trouble you?
For if I break, you may mistrust
The Vow I made to love you too.

SONG VII.

Alexis shun'd his fellow Swains,
Their rural Sports, and jocund Strains,
(Heaven guard us all from Cupid's Bow!)
He lost his Crook, he left his Flocks,
And wand'ring thro' the lonely Rocks,
He nourish'd endless Woe.

The Nymphs and Shepherds round him came,
His Grief some pity, others blame,
The fatal Cause all kindly seek:
He mingled his Concern with theirs,
He gave them back their friendly Tears,
He sigh'd, but could not speak.

Clorinda came amongst the rest,
And she too, kind Concern exprest,
And ask'd the Reason of his Woe:
She ask'd, but with an Air and Mien,
As made it easily forseen
She fear'd too much to know.

The Shepherd rais'd his mournful Head,
And will you pardon me, he said,
While I the cruel Truth reveal,

Which nothing from my Breast should tear,
Which never should offend your Ear
But that you bid me tell?

'Tis thus I rove, 'tis thus complain,
Since you appeared on the Plain;
You are the Cause of all my Care:
Your Eyes ten thousand Dangers dart,
Ten thousand Torments vex my Heart;
I love and I despair.

Too much *Alexis* I have heard,
'Tis what I thought, 'tis what I fear'd;
And yet I pardon you, she cry'd:
But you shall promise ne'er again
To breathe your Vows, or speak your Pain:
He bow'd, obey'd, and dy'd.

SONG VIII.

When *Delia* on the Plain appears,
Aw'd by a thousand tender Fears,
I would approach, but dare not move;
Tell me my Heart, if this be Love.

Whene'er she speaks, my ravish'd Ear
No other Voice but her's can hear,
No other Wit but her's approve;
Tell me my Heart, if this be Love.

If she some other Swain commend,
Tho' I was once his fondest Friend,
That Instant, Enemy I prove;
Tell me my Heart, if this be Love.

When she is absent, I no more
Delight in all that pleas'd before;
The clearest Spring, or shady Grove;
Tell me my Heart, if this be Love.

When arm'd with insolent Disdain,
She seem'd to triumph o'er my Pain;
I strove to hate, but vainly strove;
Tell me my Heart, if this be Love.

SONG IX.

If *Corinna* would but hear
What impatient Love cou'd say,
She would banish idle Fear,
And with Ease his Laws obey;
She would soon approve the Song,
Like the Voice, and bless the Tongue.

Since to Silence I'm confin'd,
Sighs and Ogles must declare
What torments my thoughtful Mind;
How I wish, and how despair:
All the Motions of my Heart,
Sighs and Ogles must impart.

SONG X.

Were I to choose the greatest Bliss
That e'er in Love was known,
'Twould be the highest of my Wish
T' enjoy her Heart alone.

Kings might possess their Kingdoms free,
And Crowns unenvied wear,
They should no Rival have of me,
Might I reign a Monarch there.

Hear, *Cynthia*, hear the gentle Air,
But whisper out my Love,
And prove but half so kind as fair,
My Sorrow you'll remove.

Cynthia, oh! let us happy be,
Unite our Hearts in Love;
I'd change not such Felicity,
For all the Joys above.

SONG XI.

When first I saw her graceful move,
Ah me, what meant my throbbing Breast?
Say, soft Confusion, art thou Love?
If Love thou art, then farewell Rest!

Since doom'd I am to love the Fair,
Though hopeless of a warm Return,
Yet kill me not with cold Despair,
But let me live, and let me burn.

With gentle Smiles assuage the Pain,
Those gentle Smiles did first create;
And though you cannot love again,
In pity, oh, forbear to hate.

SONG XII.

Charming *Cloe*, look with Pity
On your faithful, Love-sick Swain:
Hear, oh hear his doleful Ditty,
And relieve his mighty Pain:
Find you Musick in his sighing,
Can you see him in Distress,
Wishing, trembling, panting, dying,
Yet afford no kind Redress?

Strephon woo'd by lawless Passion,
For no Favours rudely sues;
All his Flame is out of Fashion,
Ancient Honour from him woos.
Love for Love's the Swain's Ambition,
But if that is deem'd too great,
Pity, pity his Condition,
Say at least you do not hate.

Shou'd you, fonder of a Rover,
Practis'd in the Art of Guile,
Slight so true and kind a Lover,
Cloe, might not *Strephon* smile?
Yes: well pleas'd at thy undoing,
Vulgar Lovers might upbraid;
Strephon, conscious of thy Ruin,
Soon wou'd be a silent Shade.

SONG XIII.

Where would coy *Aminta* run,
From a despairing Lover's Story?
When her Eyes have Conquests won,
Why should her Ear refuse the Glory?

Shall a Slave whom Racks constrain,
Be forbidden to complain?

Let her scorn me, let her fly me,
Let her Looks her Love deny me;
Ne'er can my Heart change for Relief,
Or my Tongue cease to tell my Grief;
Much to Love and much to Pray,
Is to Heaven the only Way.

SONG XIV.

I did but look and love a while,
'Twas but for one half Hour;
Then to resist I had no Will,
And now I have no Power.

To sigh, and wish, is all my Ease;
Sighs which do Heat impart,
Enough to melt the coldest Ice,
Yet cannot warm your Heart.

Oh! would your Pity give my Heart
One corner of your Breast;
'Twould learn of yours the winning Art,
And quickly steal the rest.

SONG XV.

Tho', *Phyllis*, you scorn my Address,
Preferring a Rattle that's vain;
Yet know 'tis Respect in Excess,
My Freedom of Speech does restrain.
O cruel! consider my Fire
Burns fiercer the more 'tis depress'd,
While his in a Flash does expire;
He talks of a Passion in jest.

How oft I've resolv'd when alone,
In fittest Words that I cou'd choose,
My Affection so true to make known
But Speech in your Presence I lose:
Still what I am going to say,
Seems foolish, ridiculous Stuff;
My Thoughts in a Chaos do play;
No Expressions are worthy enough.

O, fairest, your **Servant** believe,
This is of true Love the Effect;
And what greater Proof can he give?
For where there is Love there's Respect.
All Scholars in Young Cupid's School
The Rhet'rick of Tongues still despise;
'Tis in Am'rous Converse a Rule,
To talk the soft Language of Eyes.

SONG XVI.

Phillis, Men say that all my Vows
Are to thy Fortune paid:
Alas! my Heart he little knows,
Who thinks my Love a Trade.

Were I of all these Woods the Lord,
One Berry from thy Hand
More real Pleasure wou'd afford
Than all my large Command.

My humble Love has learnt to live
On what the nicest Maid,
Without a conscious Blush, may give
Beneath a Myrtle Shade.

Of costly Food it hath no need,
And nothing will devour:
But, like the harmless Bee, can feed,
And not impair the Flow'r.

A spotless Innocence like thine,
May such a Flame allow;
Yet thy fair Name for ever shine,
As doth thy Beauty now.

SONG XVII.

The Bird that hears her Nestlings cry,
And flies abroad for Food,
Returns impatient through the Sky,
To nurse the Callow Brood.

The tender Mother knows no Joy,
But boads a thousand Harms,
And sickens for the darling Boy,
While absent from her Arms.

Such Fondness, with Impatience join'd,
My faithful Bosom fires;
Now forc'd to leave my Fair behind,
The Queen of my Desires!

The Powers of Verse too languid prove,
All Similies are vain
To show how ardently I love,
Or to relieve my Pain.

The Saint with fervent Zeal inspir'd
For Heaven and Joys divine,
The Saint is not with Raptures fir'd
More pure, more warm, than mine.

I take what Liberty I dare,
'Twere impious to say more.
Convey my Longings to the Fair,
The Goddess I adore.

SONG XVIII.

Tell me not, I my Time mispend,
'Tis Time lost to reprove me,
Pursue thou thine, I have my End,
So *Cloris* only love me.

Tell me not other Flocks are full,
Mine poor, let them despise me,
Who more abound with Milk and Wool,
So *Cloris* only prize me.

Tire others easier Ears with these
Unappertaining Stories;
He never felt the World's Disease,
Who cared not for its Glories.

For Pity, thou that wiser art,
Whose Thoughts lye wide of mine;
Let me alone with all my Heart,
And I'll ne'er envy thine.

Nor blame him who e'er blames my Wit,
That seeks no higher Prize,
Than in unenvi'd Shades to sit,
And sing of *Chloris'* Eyes.

SONG XIX.

For many unsuccessful Years,
At *Cynthia's* Feet I lay;
Batt'ring them often with my Tears,
I sigh'd but must not pray.
No prostrate Wretch before the Shrine
Of some lov'd Saint above,
E'er thought his Goddess more divine,
Or paid more awful Love.

Still the disdainful Nymph looked down,
With coy, insulting Pride;
Received my Passion with a Frown,
Or turn'd her Head aside.
Then *Cupid* whisper'd in my Ear,
Use more prevailing Charms;
You modest whining Fool, draw near,
And clasp her in your Arms:

With eager Kisses tempt the Maid;
From *Cynthia's* Feet depart;
The Lips he briskly must invade,
That wou'd possess the Heart.
With that I shook off all the Slave,
My better Fortunes try'd;
When *Cynthia* in a Moment gave
What she for Years deny'd.

SONG XX.

A gentle Warmth comes o'er my Heart,
Short pleasing Sighs to blow the Fire;
Beauty and Youth can ne'er want Art,
To heighten eager Love's Desire.

I sigh and she trembles,
Yet her Eyes shew some Joy,
Which she'd fain dissemble
By seeming more coy.

Pr'ythee be no more coy,
Pr'ythee, *Cynthia* my dear,
We were made to enjoy
The sweet Pleasure we fear.

SONG XXI.

As *Clintor* and *Amelia* sat,
He (simple Swain) in idle Chat,
And useless Talk, the Time mispent;
Which to their mutual, great Content,
(Had Modesty but left the Boy)
Had been employ'd in mutual Joy.

Her Lips, her Eyes, her Breasts he prais'd,
Whilst every Charm new Transports rais'd:
Transports of Tongue; for that alone
Made all his Joys and Transport known;
Dull Joys! dull Transports! duller Boy!
That could such Time so ill employ.

SONG XXII.

At Break of Day, poor *Celadon*,
Hard by his Sheep-folds walk'd alone;
His Arms a-cross, his Head bow'd down,
His oaten Pipe beside him thrown;
When *Thersis*, hidden in a Thicket by,
Thus heard the discontented Shepherd cry:

What is it *Celadon* has done,
That all his Happiness is gone?
The Curtains of the Dark are drawn,
And chearful Morn begins to dawn;
Yet in my Breast 'tis ever dead of Night,
That can admit no Beam of pleasant Light.

Yon pretty Lambs do leap and play,
To welcome the new kindled Day;
Your Shepherd harmless, as are you,
Why is he not as frolick too?
If such Disturbance th' Innocent attend,
How differs he from them that dare offend?

Ye Gods! or let me die, or live;
If I must die, why this Reprieve?
If you would have me live, O why
Is it with me as those that die?
I faint, I gasp, I pant, my Eyes are set,
My Cheeks are pale, and I am living yet.

Ye Gods! I never did withhold
The fattest Lamb of all my Fold,
But on your Altars laid it down,
And with a Garland did it crown.
Is it in vain to make your Altars smoke?
Is it all one, to please and to provoke?

Time was that I could sit and smile,
Or with a Dance the Time beguile;
My Soul, like that smooth Lake, was still,
Bright as the Sun behind yon Hill;
Like yonder stately Mountain clear and high,
Swift, soft, and gay, as that same Butterfly.

But now within there's Civil War,
In Arms my rebel Passions are,
Their old Allegiance laid aside,
The Traytors now in Triumph ride;
That many-headed Monster has thrown down
Its lawful Monarch, Reason, from his Throne.

See, unrelenting *Sylvia*, see
All this, and more, is long of thee;
For ere I saw that charming Face
Uninterrupted was my Peace;
Thy glorious beamy Eyes have struck me blind,
To my own Soul the Way I cannot find.

Yet is it not thy Fault, nor mine;
Heav'n is to blame, that did not shine
Upon us both with equal Rays;
It made thine bright, mine gloomy Days.
To *Sylvia* Beauty gave, and Riches' Store,
All *Celadon's* Offense is he is poor.

Unlucky Stars poor Shepherds have,
Whose Love is fickle Fortune's Slave:
Those Golden Days are out of Date,
When every Turtle chose his Mate:
Cupid, that mighty Prince, then uncontroul'd,
Now like a little Negro's bought and sold.

SONG XXIII.

At Noon in a Sun-shiny Day,
The brightest Lady of the May,
Yong *Cloris*, innocent and gay,
Set Knotting in a Shade.

Each slender Finger play'd its Part,
With such Activity and Art,
As wou'd inflame a youthful Heart,
And warm the most decay'd.

Her fav'rite Swain by chance came by—
He saw no Anger in her Eye;
Yet when the bashful Boy drew nigh,
She wou'd have seem'd afraid.

She let her Ivory Needle fall,
And hurl'd away the twisted Ball:
But straight gave *Strephon* such a call,
As would have raised the Dead.

Dear gentle Youth, is't none but thee?
With Innocence I dare be free;
By so much Truth and Modesty,
No Nymph was e'er betrayed.

Come lean thy Head upon my Lap,
While thy smooth Cheeks I stroke and clap;
Thou may'st securely take a Nap:
Which he poor Fool obey'd.

She saw him Yawn, and heard him Snore,
And found him fast asleep all o'er;
She sigh'd and cou'd endure no more,
But, starting up she said;

Such Virtue shall rewarded be;
For this thy dull Fidelity
I'll trust thee with my Flocks, not me:
Pursue thy grazing Trade.

Go milk thy Goats, and shear thy Sheep,
And watch all Night thy Flocks to keep;
Thou shalt no more be lull'd asleep
By me, mistaken Maid.

SONG XXIV.

Over the Mountains,
And over the Waves;
Over the Fountains,
And under the Graves;

Over Floods that are deepest,
Which do *Neptune* obey;
Over Rocks that are steepest,
Love will find out the Way.

Wher there **is no Place**
For the Glowworm to ly;
Wher there is no Space
For Receit of a Fly;
Wher the Midge dares not venture
Lest herself fast she lay;
But if Love come, he will enter,
And soon find out his Way.

**You may esteem him
A Child in his Force;
Or you may deem him
A Coward, which is worse:**
But if she, whom Love doth honour,
Be conceal'd from the Day,
Set a thousand Guards upon her,
Love will find out the Way.

Some think **to** lose him,
Which is **too** unkind;
And some **do** suppose him,
Poor Thing, to be blind;
But if ne'er so close ye wall him,
Do the best that ye may,—
Blind Love, if so ye call him,
He will find out the Way.

You may train the Eagle
To stoop to your Fist;
Or **you** may inveagle
The Phaenix of the East!
The Lioness, ye may move her
To give over her Prey:
But **you'll never stop a Lover,**
He will find out the Way.

THE CONSTANT LOVER.

SONG I.

You I love, by all that's true,
More than all things here below;
With a Passion far more great
Than e'er Creature loved yet;
And yet still you cry forbear,
Love no more, or love not here.

Bid the Miser leave his Ore;
Bid the Wretched sigh no more;
Bid the Old be young again;
Bid the Nun not think of Man:
Silvia when you this can do,
Bid me then not think of you.

Love's not a Thing of Choice, but Fate;
What makes me love, makes you to hate;
Silvia then do what you will,
Ease, or cure, torment, or kill;
Be kind or cruel, false or true,
Love I must, and none but you.

SONG II.

Tell me, tell me, charming Creature,
Will you never ease my Pain?
Must I die for every Feature?
Must I always love in vain?
The Desire of Admiration,
Is the Pleasure you pursue;
Prithee try a lasting Passion,
Such a Love as mine for you.

Tears and Sighing could not move you,
For a Lover ought to dare;
When I plainly told I lov'd you,
Then you said I went too far.

Are such giddy ways beseeming?
Will my Dear be fickle still?
Conquest is the Joy of Women,
Let their Slaves be what they will.

Your Neglect with Torment fills me,
And my desperate Thoughts encrease;
Pray consider if you kill me,
You will have a Lover less.
If your wandering Heart is beating
For new Lovers, let it be:
But when you have done coquetting,
Name a Day, and fix on me.

SONG III.

All Thoughts of Freedom are too late,
Not any new fair Lady's Art,
Nor both the *India's* Wealth, nor Fate
Itself can disengage my Heart.

Not which kind Heaven forbid! your Hate,
And that which follows proud Disdain,
My Passion cou'd at all abate,
But only make it last with Pain.

Thus all my Quiet does depend
On Hopes t'obtain a Smile from you;
That so my Love, that knows no End,
May last with equal Pleasure too.

SONG IV.

Give over, foolish Heart, and make haste to despair,
For *Daphne* regards not thy Vows, nor thy Pray'r:
When I plead for thy Passion, thy Pains to prolong,
She courts her Guittar, and replies with a Song;
No more shall true Lovers thy Beauty adore;
Were the Gods so severe, Men wou'd worship no more.

No more will I wait like a Slave at thy Door,
I'll spend the cold Nights at thy Window no more;
My Lungs in cold Sighs I no more will exhale,
Since thy Pride is to make me look sullen and pale;
No more shall *Amyntas* thy Pity implore;
Were the Gods so ingrate, Men wou'd worship no more.

No more shall thy Frowns, or free Humour persuade,
To court the fair Idol my Fancy has made;
When thy Saints so neglected their Follies give o'er,
Thy Deity's lost, and thy Beauty's no more.

How weak are the Vows of a Lover in Pain,
When flatter'd by Hope, or oppress'd by Disdain;
No sooner my *Daphne's* bright Eyes I review,
But all is forgot, and I vow all anew.
No more, cruel Nymph, I will murmur no more;
Did the Gods seem so fair, Men wou'd worship them more.

SONG V.

The last Time I came o'er the Moor,
I left my Love behind me;
Ye Gods! what Pain do I endure,
When soft Ideas mind me?
Soon as the ruddy Morn display'd
The beaming Day ensuing,
I met betimes my lovely Maid,
In fit Retreats for Wooing.

Beneath the cooling Shades we lay,
Gazing and chastely Sporting;
We kissed and promis'd Time away
Till Night spread her black Curtain.
I pitied all beneath the Skies,
Ev'n Kings, when she was nigh me:
In Raptures I beheld her Eye,
Which could but ill deny me.

Should I be call'd where Cannons,
Where mortal Steel may wound me;
Or cast upon some Foreign Shore,
Where Dangers may surround me,
Yet Hopes again to see my Love,
To feast on glowing Kisses,
Shall make my Cares at Distance move,
In prospect of such Blisses.

In all my Soul there's not one Place
To let a Rival enter;
Since she excels in every Grace,
In her my Love shall center.

Sooner the Seas shall cease to flow,
Their Waves the *Alps* shall cover;
On Greenland's Ice shall Roses blow,
Before I cease to love her.

SONG VI.

Sweet are the Charms of her I love,
More fragrant than the damask Rose;
Soft as the Down of Turtle Dove,
Gentle as Winds when Zephir blows,
Refreshing as descending Rains,
To Sun-burnt Climes, and thirsty **Plains.**

True as the Needle to the Pole,
Or as the Dial to the Sun,
Constant as gliding Waters roll,
Whose swelling Tides obey the Moon:
From every other Charmer free,
My Life and **Love** shall follow thee.

The Lamb of flow'ry Thyme devours,
The Dam the tender Kid pursues;
Sweet *Philomel* in shady Bowers,
With verdant Spring, her Notes renews:
All follow what they most admire,
As I pursue my Soul's Desire.

Nature must change her beauteous **Face,**
And vary as the Seasons rise;
As Winter to the Spring gives Place,
Summer th' approach of Autumn flies;
No change on Love the Seasons bring,
Love only **knows** perpetual Spring.

Devouring Time with stealing Pace
Makes lofty Oaks and Cedars bow;
And Marble Towers, and Walls of Brass,
In his rude March he levels low;
But **Time,** destroying far and wide,
Love from the Soul **can** ne'er divide.

Death only, with his cruel **Dart,**
The gentle Godhead **can** remove;
And drive **him from the** bleeding Heart,
To mingle with **the** Blest above;
When known to all his Kindred Train,
He finds a lasting Rest from Pain.

Love and his Sister fair, the Soul,
Twin-born from Heaven together came;
Love will the Universe controul,
When dying Seasons lose their Name:
Divine Abodes shall own his Power,
When Time and Death shall be no more.

SONG VII.

Fair *Cloe* my Breast so alarms,
From her Pow'r no Refuge I find;
If another I take to my Arms,
Yet my *Cloe* is then in my Mind;
Unblest with the Joy, still a Pleasure I want,
Which none but my *Cloe*, my *Cloe* can grant.

Let *Cloe* but smile, I grow gay,
And I feel my Heart spring with Delight
On *Cloe* I could gaze all the Day,
And *Cloe* do wish for all Night.

Oh! did *Cloe* know how I love,
And the Pleasure of loving again,
My Passion her Favour would move,
And in Prudence she'd pity my Pain:
Good Nature and Int'rest shou'd both make her kind,
For the Joy she might give, and the Joy she might find.

SONG VIII.

Lost is my Quiet for ever;
Lost is Life's happiest Part;
Lost all my tender Endeavour
To touch an insensible Heart.

But tho' my Despair is past curing,
And much undeserved is my Fate;
I'll shew, by a patient Enduring,
My Love is unmov'd as her Hate.

SONG IX.

I cannot change, as others do,
Tho' you unjustly scorn:
Since that poor Swain that sighs for you,
For you alone was born.

No *Phillis*, no, your Heart to move
A surer way I'll try;
And to revenge my slighted Love,
Will still love on, will still love on and die.

When, kill'd with Grief, *Amintas* lies,
And you to mind shall call
The Sighs that now unpity'd rise,
The Tears that vainly fall.

That welcome Hour that ends this Smart,
Will then begin your Pain;
For such a faithful tender Heart
Can never break, can never break in vain.

SONG X.

In vain, dear *Cloe*, you suggest
That I, inconstant, have posses't,
Or loved a fairer She:
But if at once you wou'd be cur'd
Of all the Ills you have endur'd,
Look in your Glass and see.

And if perchance you then should find,
A Nymph more lovely or more kind,
You've Reason for your Tears:
But if impartial you will prove,
Both to your Beauty and my Love,
How needless are those Fears.

If in my Way I should, by Chance,
Give or receive a wanton Glance,
I like but whilst I view:
How faint the Glance, how slight the Kiss,
Compared to that substantial Bliss,
I still receive from you.

With wanton Flight the curious Bee,
From Flow'r to Flow'r still wanders free;
And where each Blossom blows,
Extracts the Juice of all he meets,
And for his Quintessence of Sweets,
He ravishes the Rose.

So I, my Leisure to employ,
In each Variety of Joy,
From Nymph to Nymph do roam;
Perhaps see fifty in a Day;
They are but Visits which I pay,
For *Cloe's* still my Home.

SONG XI.

Iris, your lovely fatal Eyes
Command such pow'rful Darts,
No wonder if you one despise,
To wound a thousand Hearts.

But cou'd you guess the vast **Delight**
To constant Lovers known,
You wou'd your thousand Conquests slight,
And rule my Heart alone.

SONG XII.

Dear *Cloe*, while thus beyond Measure,
You treat me with Doubts and Disdain,
You rob all your Youth of its Pleasure,
And hoard up an old Age of Pain:
Your Maxim, That Love is but founded
On Charms that will quickly decay;
You'll be very ill grounded,
When once you its Dictates obey.

The Passion from Beauty first drawn,
Your Kindness wou'd vastly improve;
Your Sight and your Smiles are the Dawn,
Fruition's the Sun-shine of Love:
And tho' the bright Beams of your **Eyes**
Shou'd be clouded, that now are so gay,
And Darkness possess all the Skies,
Yet we ne'er can forget it was Day.

Old Darby, with Joan by his side,
You've often regarded with Wonder:
He's dropsical, she is sore-eyed,
Yet they're ever uneasy asunder:

Together they totter about,
Or sit in the Sun at the Door,
And at Night when old Darby's Pipe's out,
His Joan will not smoke a Whiff more.

No Beauty nor Wit they possess,
Their several Failings to smother;
Then, what are the Charms, can you guess,
That make them so fond of each other?
'Tis the pleasing Remembrance of Youth,
The Endearments which Youth did bestow,
The Thoughts of past Pleasure and Truth,
The best of our Blessings below.

Those Traces for ever will last,
Which Sickness and Time can't remove;
For when Youth and Beauty are past,
And Age brings the *Winter of Love*,
A Friendship insensible grows,
By Reviews of such Raptures as these;
The Current of Fondness still flows,
Which decrepid old Age cannot freeze.

SONG XIII.

Dejected as true Converts die,
But yet with fervent Thoughts inflam'd;
So, Fairest, at your Feet I lie,
Of all my Sex's Faults asham'd.

Too long alas! have I defy'd
The Force of Love's almighty Flame;
And often did aloud deride
His God-head, as an empty Name.

But since so freely I confess
A Crime, which may your Scorn produce,
Allow me now to make it less,
By any just and fair Excuse.

I then did vulgar Joys pursue,
Variety was all my Bliss;
But ignorant of Love and you,
How could I chuse but do amiss?

If ever now my wand'ring Eyes
Search out Temptations as before;
If once I look, but to despise
Their Charms, and value yours the more;

May sad **Remorse,** and guilty Shame,
Revenge your Wrongs on faithless me ;
And what I tremble ev'n to name,
May I lose all, in losing thee.

SONG XIV.

Believe my Sighs, my Tears, my Dear,
Believe the Heart you've won :
Believe my Vows to you sincere,
Or *Moggy,* I'm undone.
You say I'm fickle, and apt to change
At ev'ry Face that's new ;
But of all the Girls I ever saw,
I ne'er lov'd one but you.

My Heart was but a Lump of Ice,
'Till warm'd by your bright Eyes ;
But ah ! they kindled in a trice
A Flame which never dies.
Come, take me, try me, and you'll find,
Tho' you say that I am not true,
Of all the Girls I ever saw,
I ne'er lov'd one but you.

SONG XV.

Gentle Love, this Hour befriend me,
To my Eyes resign thy Dart ;
Notes of melting Musick lend me,
To dissolve a frozen Heart.

Chill as Mountain Snow her **Bosom,**
Tho' I tender Language use ;
'Tis by cold Indifference frozen
To my Arms and to my Love.

See my dying Eyes are pleading,
See a broken Heart appears,
For thy Pity interceding
The Eloquence of Tears.

Whilst the Lamp of Life is fading,
And beneath thy Coldness dies,
Death by ebbing Pulse invading
Take my Soul into thy Eyes.

THE JEALOUS LOVER.

SONG I.

Away with Sorrow and Whining—
Your Rival is mighty, 'tis true :
But can there be Reason in Pining
While the Fair is constant to you?

What tho' she's in the midst of Danger,
Virtue's the Shield of her Heart ;
No Flatt'ry, no Threats, can change her,
Who's proof against Terror and Art.

The honest, the innocent, Lover
May rest, or travel, unarm'd ;
What Creature will venture to move her,
By whom the Creation is charm'd?

When *Horace* was heedless straying,
In his *Sabinean* Grove,
A Wolf, intent upon preying,
Pass'd by and did Homage to Love.

SONG II.

Too lovely, cruel Fair,
Can I the Torture bear
To see thee flying?
Must I behold those Charms
Doom'd to another's Arms,
While I am dying?

SONG III.

Oh conceal that charming Creature
From my wond'ring wishing Eyes!
Every Motion, every Feature
Does some ravished Heart surprize ;

But oh, I sighing, sighing, see
The happy Swain! she ne'er can be
False to him, or kind to me.

Yet if I could humbly show her,
Ah! how wretched I remain;
'Tis not, sure, a Thing below her,
Still to pity so much Pain;
The Gods some Pleasure, Pleasure take,
Happy as themselves to make
Those who suffer for their sake.

Since your Hand alone was giv'n
To a Wretch not worth your Care;
Like some Angel sent from Heav'n
Come and raise me from Despair:
Your Heart I cannot, cannot miss,
And I desire no other Bliss;
Let all the World beside be his.

SONG IV.

A Swain of Love despairing,
Thus wail'd his cruel Fate;
His Grief the Shepherds sharing,
In Circles round him sat:
The Nymphs in kind Compassion,
The luckless Lover mourn'd;
All who had felt the Passion,
A Sigh for Sigh return'd.

Oh! Friends! your Plaints give over,
Your kind Concern forbear;
Should *Cloe* but discover
For me you've shed a Tear,
Her Eyes she'd arm with Vengeance,
Your Friendship soon subdue;
Too late you ask Forgiveness,
And for her Mercy sue.

Her Charms such Force discover,
Resistance is in vain;
Spite of yourself you'll love her,
And hug the galling Chain.
Her Wit the Flame increases,
And rivets fast the Dart;
She has ten thousand Graces,
And each could gain a Heart.

But oh! one more deserving
Has thaw'd her frozen Breast;
Her Heart to him devoting,
She's cold to all the rest.
Their Love with Joy abounding,
The Thought distracts my Brain;
Oh! cruel Maid—then swooning,
He fell upon the Plain.

SONG V.

Charming is your Shape and Air,
And your Face as Morning fair;
Coral Lips, and Neck of Snow,
Cheeks where opening Roses blow;
When you speak, or smile, or move,
All is Rapture, all is Love.

But those Eyes, alas! I hate!
Eyes that, heedless of my Fate,
Shine with undiscerning Rays;
On the Fopling idly gaze;
Watch the Glances of the Vain;
Meeting mine with cold Disdain.

SONG VI.

My dear Mistress has a Heart,
Soft as those kind Looks she gave me,
When with Love's resistless Art,
And her Eyes she did enslave me:
But her Constancy's so weak,
She's so wild, so apt to wander,
That my jealous Heart would break,
Should we live one Day asunder.

Melting Joys about her move,
Killing Pleasures, wounding Blisses;
She can dress her Eyes in Love,
And her Lips can arm with Kisses:
Angels listen when she speaks;
She's my Delight, all Mankind's Wonder;
But my jealous Heart would break,
Should we live one Day asunder.

SONG VII.

Despairing besides a clear Stream,
A Shepherd forsaken was laid;
And whilst a false Nymph was his Theme,
A Willow supported his head.
The Winds that blew over the Plain,
To his Sighs with a Sigh did reply;
And the Brook in return to his Pain,
Ran mournfully murmuring by.

Alas! silly Swain that I was,
(Thus sadly complaining he cry'd)
When first I beheld that fair Face,
'Twere better by far I had dy'd:
She talk'd and I blest her dear **Tongue**;
When she smil'd it was Pleasure **too great**;
I listened, and cry'd when she sung,
Was Nightingale ever so sweet?

How foolish **was** I to believe,
She could doat on so lowly a Clown?
Or **that** her fond Heart would not grieve
To forsake the fine Folk of the Town?
To think that a Beauty so gay,
So kind and so constant would prove,
Or go clad like our Maidens in Grey,
Or live in a Cottage on Love?

What tho' I have skill to complain,
Tho' the Muses my Temples have crown'd?
What tho' when they hear my soft Strain,
The Virgins sit weeping around?
Ah *Colin* thy Hopes are in vain,
Thy Pipe and thy Laurel resign,
Thy Fair one inclines to a Swain,
Whose Musick is sweeter than thine.

All you my Companions so dear,
Who sorrow to see me betray'd,
Whatever I suffer, forbear,
Forbear to accuse the false Maid:
Tho' thro' the wide World I should range,
'Tis in vain from my Fortune to fly;
'Twas hers to be false and to change,
'Tis mine to be constant and die.

If while my hard Fate I sustain,
In her Breast any Pity is found,
Let her come with the Nymphs of the Plain,
And see me laid low in the ground.
The last humble Boon that I crave,
Is to shade me with Cyprus and Yew,
And when she looks down on my Grave,
Let her own that her Shepherd was true.

Then to her new Love let her go,
And deck her in golden Array,
Be finest at every fine Show,
And frolick it all the long Day:
While *Colin* forgotten and gone,
No more shall be talk'd on or seen,
Unless when beneath the pale Moon,
His Ghost shall glide over the Green.

SONG VIII.

Swain, thy hopeless Passion smother,
Perjured *Celia* loves another;
In his Arms I saw her lying,
Panting, kissing, trembling, dying;
Then the fair Deceiver swore,
As she did to you before.

Oh! said you, when she deceives me,
When that constant Creature leaves me,
Isis Waters back shall fly,
And leave these oozy Channels dry;
Turn, ye Waters, leave your Shore;
Perjur'd *Celia* loves no more.

SONG IX.

What state of Life can be so blest
As Love, that warms a Lover's Breast?
Two Souls in one, the same Desire
To grant the Bliss, and to require:
But if in Heav'n a Hell we find,
'Tis all from thee,
O Jealousie!
Thou Tyrant, Tyrant Jealousie,
Thou Tyrant of the Mind.

All other Ills, tho' sharp they prove,
Serve to refine and perfect Love:
In Absence or unkind Disdain,
Sweet Hope relieves the Lover's Pain:
But ah, no cure but Death we find
To set us free
From Jealousie.
O Jealousie! &c.

False in thy Glass all Objects are,
Some set too near, and some too far;
Thou art the Fire of endless Night,
The Fire that burns, and gives no Light.
All Torments of the damn'd we find
In only thee,
O Jealousie! &c.

SONG X.

Wherever I am, and whatever I do,
My *Phillis* is still in my Mind;
When angry, I mean not to *Phillis* to go,
My Feet of themselves the Way find:
Unknown to myself I am just at her Door,
And when I would rail, I can bring out no more,
Than *Phillis* too fair and unkind!

When *Phillis* I see, my Heart burns in my Breast,
And the Love I would stifle is shown:
But asleep, or awake, I am never at Rest,
When from mine Eyes *Phillis* is gone:
Sometimes a sweet Dream doth delude my sad Mind;
But alas! when I wake, and no *Phillis* I find,
Then I sigh to myself all alone.

Should a King be my Rival in her I adore,
He shou'd offer his Treasure in vain:
O let me alone to be happy and poor,
And give me my *Phillis* again:
Let *Phillis* be mine, and but ever be kind,
I cou'd to a Desert with her be confin'd,
And envy no Monarch his Reign.

Alas, I discover too much of my Love,
And she too well knows her own Pow'r:
She makes me grow jealous each Hour.
But tho' every Moment torments my poor Mind,
I had rather love *Phillis*, both false and unkind,
Than ever be freed from her Pow'r.

SONG XI.

O Love, what cruel Pangs are these,
The cold Effect of warm Desire,
Whose agonizing Tortures freeze,
Tho' sprung from your prevailing Fire.

Her Absence gave exceeding Pain;
But when from that I hop'd Relief,
You, still resolv'd I shou'd complain,
With Jealousy augment my Grief.

Too bitter is the Lover's Part,
When sever'd from his Fair one's Eyes;
But if he's banished from her Heart,
Stabb'd with Despair at once he dies.

SONG XII.

Through mournful Shades and solitary Groves,
Fann'd with the Sighs of unsuccessful Loves,
Wild with Despair, young *Thyrsis* strays,
Thinks over all *Amyra*'s Heavenly Charms,
Thinks he now sees her in another's Arms;
Then at some Willow Root himself he lays,
The loveliest, most unhappy Swain;
And thus to the wild Woods he does complain.

How art thou chang'd, O *Thyrsis*, since the Time
When thou couldst Love, and hope without a Crime;
When Nature's Pride, and Earth's Delight,
As through her shady Ev'ning Grove she past,
And a new Day did all around her cast;
Could see, nor be offended at the Sight,
The melting, sighing, wishing Swain,
That now must never hope to wish again.

Riches and Titles! why should they prevail,
Where Duty, Love, and Adoration fail?
Lovely *Amyra* shou'dst thou prize
The empty Noise that a fine Title makes,
Or the vile Trash that with the Vulgar takes,
Before a Heart that bleeds for thee and dies?
Unkind! but pity the poor Swain
Your Rigour kills, nor triumph o'er the Slain.

THE TENDER LOVER.

SONG I.

From all uneasy Passions free,
Revenge, Ambition, Jealousie;
Contented I had been too blest,
If Love and you had let me rest:
Yet that dull Life I now despise;
Safe from your Eyes,
I fear'd no Griefs, but then I found no Joys.

Amidst a thousand kind Desires,
Which Beauty moves, and Love inspires;
Such Pangs I feel of tender Fear,
No Heart so soft as mine can bear.
Yet I'll defy the worst of Harms;
Such are your Charms,
'Tis worth a Life to die within your Arms.

SONG II.

Blest as th' immortal Gods is he,
The Youth who fondly sits by thee,
And hears and sees thee all the while,
Softly speak and sweetly smile.

'Twas this bereav'd my Soul of Rest,
And rais'd such Tumults in my Breast,
For while I gaz'd, in Transport lost,
My Breath was gone, my Voice was lost.

My Bosom glow'd, the subtle Flame
Ran quick thro' all my vital Frame,
O'er my dim Eyes a Darkness hung,
My Ears with hollow Murmurs rung.

In dewy Damps my Limbs were chill'd,
My Blood with gentle Horrors thrill'd,
My feeble Pulse forgot to play,
I fainted, sunk, and dy'd away.

SONG III.

Would Fate to me *Belinda* give,
With her alone I'd chuse to live;
Variety I'd ne'er desire,
Nor a greater, nor a greater,
Nor a greater Bliss desire.

My charming Nymph, if you can find
Amongst the Race of Human-kind
A Man that loves you more than I,
I'll resign you, I'll resign you,
I'll resign you tho' I die.

Let my *Belinda* fill my Arms,
With all her Beauties, and all her Charms,
With Scorn and Pity I'd look down
On the Glories, on the Glories,
On the Glories of a Crown.

SONG IV.

Did ever Swain a Nymph adore,
As I ungrateful *Nanny* do?
Was ever Shepherd's Heart so sore,
Or ever broken Heart so true?
My Cheeks are swell'd with Tears, but she
Has never wet a Cheek for me.

If *Nanny* call'd, did e'er I stay?
Or linger when she bid me run?
She only had a Word to say,
And all she wished was quickly done.
I always think of her, but she
Does ne'er bestow a Thought on me.

To let her Cows my Clover taste,
Have I not rose by break of Day?
Did ever *Nanny's* Heifers fast,
If *Robin* in his Barn had Hay?
Though to my Fields they welcome were,
I ne'er was welcome yet to her.

If ever *Nanny* lost a Sheep,
Then cheerfully I gave her two;
And I her Lambs did safely keep,
Within my Folds in Frost and Snow.
Have they not there from Cold been free?
But *Nanny* still is cold to me.

When *Nanny* to the Well did come,
'Twas I that did her Pitchers fill;
Full as they were I brought them home;
Her Corn I carri'd to the Mill:
My Back did bear the Sack, but she
Will never bear the Sight of me.

To *Nanny's* Poultry Oats I gave;
I'm sure they always had the best:
Within this Week her Pidgeons have
Eat up a Peck of Pease at least;
Her little Pidgeons kiss, but she
Will never take a Kiss from me.

Must *Robin* always *Nanny* woo,
And *Nanny* still on *Robin* frown?
Alas! poor Wretch! what shall I do
If *Nanny* does not love me soon?
If no Relief to me she'll bring,
I'll hang me in her Apron-string.

SONG V.

Why cruel Creature, why so bent
To vex a tender Heart?
To Gold and Title you relent;
Love throws away his Dart.

Let glitt'ring Fools in Court be great;
For Pay let Armies move;
Beauty shou'd have no other Bait,
But gentle Vows and Love.

If on those endless Charms you lay
The Value that's their due,
Kings are themselves too poor to pay,
A thousand Worlds too few.

But if a Passion without Vice,
Without Disguise or Art,
Ah *Celia!* if true Love's your Price,
Behold it in my Heart.

SONG VI.

Tho' cruel you seem to my Pain,
And hate me because I am true;
Yet, *Phillis*, you love a false Swain,
Who has other Nymphs in his View:
Enjoyment's a Trifle to him,
To me what a Heav'n it would be;
To him but a Woman you seem,
But, ah! you're an Angel to me!

Those Lips which he touches in Haste,
I to them for ever should grow,
Still clinging around that dear Waste,
Which he spans as beside him you go.
That Arm, like a Lilly so white,
Which over his Shoulder you lay,
My Bosom could warm it all Night,
My Lips they would press it all Day.

Were I like a Monarch to reign,
Were Graces my Subjects to be,
I'd leave them and fly to the Plain;
To dwell in a Cottage with thee:
But if I must feel thy Disdain,
If Tears cannot Cruelty drown,
O! let me not live in this Pain,
But give me my Death in a Frown.

SONG VII.

Ye Nymphs, who frequent those sweet Plains,
Where *Thames's* gentle Current doth glide;
Who, whilom, have heard my glad Strains,
Nor greatful Attention deny'd:
With Pity, ye Fair, O reflect
On cruel Reserve of my Fate;
See Constancy paid with Neglect,
And Fondness rewarded with Hate.

How joyous and gay was each Hour!
How wing'd with soft Pleasure they fled!
E'er shipwreck'd on Humber's dull Shore
By Love my poor Heart was betray'd:
For there the Deceiver doth dwell,
Whose Charms have so long been my Theme;
In Beauty the Maid doth excel,
But is fickle and wild as the Stream.

If, averse to my Courtship at first,
She had check'd my fond Infant Desire,
Her Coldness had left me less curst,
And perhaps had extinguish'd my Fire:
But a thousand false Arts she employ'd,
(Ingenious and wanton in Ill)
The Passion she nurs'd, she destroy'd,
And only created to kill.

Yet tho' she delights in my Smart,
Tho' she robs me of all I hold dear,
Revenge is below a great Heart,
I wish her a lot less severe:
May the Swain she shall crown with Success,
By his Kindness deserve to be priz'd;
'Twould double, methinks, my Distress,
At last to see her too despised.

SONG VIII.

Adieu, ye pleasant Sports and Plays,
Farewel each Song that was diverting;
Love tunes my Pipe to mournful Lays;
I sing of *Delia* and *Damon's* Parting.

Long had he lov'd, and long conceal'd
The dear tormenting pleasing Passion,
Till *Delia's* Mildness had prevail'd
On him to shew his Inclination.

Just as the Fair One seem'd to give
A patient Ear to his Love Story,
Damon must his lov'd *Delia* leave,
To go in quest of toilsome Glory.

Half-spoken Words hung on each Tongue,
Their Eyes refus'd their usual Meeting;
And Sighs supply'd their wonted Song,
These charming Sounds were chang'd to Weeping.

Dear Idol of my Soul, adieu;
Cease to lament, but ne'er to love me;
While *Damon* lives, he lives for you,
No other Charms shall ever move me.

Alas! who knows, when parted far
From *Delia*, but you may deceive her;
The Thought destroys my Heart with Care;
Adieu, my dear, I fear, for ever!

If ever I forget my Vows,
May then my Guardian Angel leave me;
And, more to aggravate my Woes,
Be you so good as to forgive me.

SONG IX.

Young *Damon*, once the happiest Swain,
The Pride and Glory of the Plain,
(Yet see the Effects of Love!)
Depriv'd of all his former Rest,
Shun'd Company, with Grief opprest,
And sought the thickest Grove.

The Nymphs and Swains all strove to find
What 'twas disturb'd the Shepherd's Mind;
And, when they begg'd to know,
He only shook his drooping Head,
And sighing mournfully, he said,
My Fate will have it so.

Myrtillo, hearing of his Woes,
Came too, and kindly ask'd the Cause
Of all his mighty Pain:
The Youth, transported, and amaz'd
To hear her charming Voice, soon rais'd
His Head, and thus began:

I love; but 'tis a Nymph so fair,
That I of all Success despair,
And nought expect but Scorn;
But, oh! forgive since ask'd by you,
If farther I my Tale pursue,
And say, for you I burn.

The Nymph then blush'd, and smiling said,
And is it thus you court a Maid?
You'll by Experience find,
The Fair's not won by dull Despair,
But to the Brave and *Debonnaire*
Our Sex will e'er prove kind.

SONG X.

By a murmuring Stream a fair Shepherdess lay;
Be so kind, O ye Nymphs, I ofttimes heard her say,
Tell *Strephon*, I die, if he passes this Way,
And that Love is the Cause of my Mourning.

False Shepherds, that tell me of Beauty and Charms,
Ye deceive me; for *Strephon's* cold Heart never warms;
Yet bring me this *Strephon*, let me die in his Arms:
Oh! *Strephon* the Cause of my mourning.

   But first, said she, let me go
   Down to the Shades below,
   E'er ye let *Strephon* know
   That I have lov'd him so;
Then on my pale Cheek no Blushes will show,
That Love was the Cause of my mourning.

Her Eyes were scarce closed when *Strephon* came by,
He thought she'd been sleeping, and softly drew nigh;
But, finding her breathless, Oh Heav'ns! did he cry,
Ah! *Cloris*, the Cause of my mourning.

Restore me my *Cloris*; ye Nymphs, use your Art;
They sighing reply'd, 'Twas yourself shot the Dart,
That wounded the tender young Shepherdess' Heart,
And kill'd the poor *Cloris* with mourning.

   Ah then is *Cloris* dead,
   Wounded by me! he said:
   I'll follow thee, chaste Maid,
   Down to the silent Shade.
Then on her cold snowy Breast leaning his Head,
Expir'd the poor *Strephon* with mourning.

SONG XI.

I'll range around the shady Bowers,
And gather all the sweetest Flowers;
I'll strip the Gardens, and the Grove,
To make a Garland for my Love.

When in the sultry Heat of Day,
My thirsty Nymph does panting lie,
I'll hasten to the Fountain's Brink,
And drain the Stream that she may drink.

At Night, when she shall weary prove,
A grassy Bed I'll make my Love,
And with green Boughs I'll form a Shade,
That nothing may her Rest invade.

And whilst dissolv'd in Sleep she lies,
Myself shall never close these Eyes,

But gazing still with fond Delight,
I'll watch my Charmer all the Night.

And then as soon as chearful Day
Dispels the gloomy Shades away,
Forth to the Forest I'll repair,
And find Provision for my Dear.

Thus will I spend the Day and Night,
Attending on her with Delight,
Regarding nothing I endure,
So I can Ease for her procure.

But if the Nymph whom thus I love,
Should ever false or faithless prove,
I'll seek some dismal, distant Shore,
And never think on Woman more.

SONG XII.

The Pain which tears my throbbing Breast,
What Language can deplore;
For how shou'd Language have exprest
A Pain ne'er felt before:
In other Virgins' wounded Hearts,
Love's cruel Sport we see,
But the most cruel of his Darts,
He has reserv'd for me.

Thy Curse, O *Tantalus!* I'd prize;
Thy Curse a Bliss would prove;
Ah! Heav'n were kind, if with my Eyes
I could enjoy my Love.
Inchanted thus, Romances tell
The Moans poor Virgins make;
But where is found the powerful Spell
Can this Inchantment break?

SONG XIII.

Had I the World at my command,
And own'd the Wealth of Sea and Land,
To *Flora* I'd present it all,
And at her Feet lay down the Ball.

Or was my Life by Scraps sustained,
From Door to Door by begging gain'd,

Would she be mine, I'd bless my Fate,
Nor wish a more exalted State.

Possessing her, or rich, or poor,
What is there to desire more?
There's nothing precious but her Charms,
And Pleasure dwells but in her Arms.

O grant, ye Pow'rs! the Fair I love,
May to my Vows propitious prove;
And from your Altars shall arise
The Smoke of daily Sacrifice.

Among the Blessings you bestow
On craving Mortals here below,
Make but the lovely Maiden mine,
I'll all the rest with Joy resign.

SONG XIV.

Oh! happy, happy Grove!
Witness of our tender Love.
O! happy, happy Shade!
Where first our Vows were made:
Blushing, sighing, melting, dying,
Looks would charm a *Jove:*
A thousand pretty Things she said,
And all—and all was Love.

But *Corinna* perjur'd proves,
And forsakes the shady Groves:
When I speak of mutual Joys,
She knows not what I mean:
Wanton Glances, fond Caresses,
Now no more are seen,
Since the false deluding Fair
Has left the flow'ry Green.

Mourn, ye Nymphs that sporting play'd,
When poor *Strephon* was betray'd;
There the secret Wound she gave,
And I was made her Slave.

SONG XV.

What shall I do to shew how much I love her?
How many millions of Sighs can suffice?
That which wins other Hearts, never can move her;
Those common Methods of Love she'll despise.

I will love **more** than Man e'er lov'd before me,
Gaze on her all the Day, melt all the Night;
Till for her own sake, at last she'll implore me,
To love her less to preserve **our** Delight.

Since Gods themselves cannot ever be loving,
Men must have breathing Recruits for new Joys;
I wish my Love could be always improving;
Tho' eager Love more than Sorrow destroys.

In fair *Aurelia's* Arms leave me expiring,
To be embalm'd by the Sweets of her Breath;
To the last Moment I'll still be desiring:
Never had Hero **so** glorious a Death.

SONG XVI.

Ye Shepherds **and** Nymphs, that adorn the gay Plain,
Approach from your Sports, and attend to my Strain;
Amongst all your Number, a Lover so true
Was ne'er so undone, with such Bliss in his View.

Was ever a Nymph so hard-hearted as mine?
She knows me sincere, and she **sees** how I pine;
She does not disdain me, nor frown in her Wrath,
But calmly, and mildly, resigns me to Death.

She calls me her Friend, but her Lover denies;
She smiles when I'm chearful, but hears not my **Sighs**:
A Bosom so flinty, so gentle an Air,
Inspires me with Hope, and yet bids **me despair**!

I fall at her Feet, and implore her with Tears;
Her Answer confounds, while her Manner indears;
When softly she tells me to hope no Relief,
My trembling Lips bless her, in spite of my Grief.

By Night while I slumber, still haunted with Care,
I start up in Anguish, and sigh for the Fair:
The Fair sleeps in Peace; may she ever do so!
And only when dreaming imagine my **Woe**.

Then gaze at a Distance, no further aspire,
Nor think she should love whom she cannot admire;
Hush all thy Complaining, and dying her Slave,
Commend her to Heav'n and thyself to the Grave.

SONG XVII.

If Love's a sweet Passion, why does it torment?
If a bitter, O tell me whence comes my Complaint?
Since I suffer with Pleasure, why should I complain?
Or grieve at my Fate, since I know 'tis in vain?
Yet so pleasing the Pain is, so soft is the Dart,
That at once it both wounds me and tickles my Heart.

I grasp her Hand gently, look languishing down,
And by passionate Silence, I make my Love known.
But oh! how I'm bless'd when so kind she does prove,
By some willing Mistake to discover her Love;
When in striving to hide, she reveals all her Flame,
And our Eyes tell each other what neither dare name.

How pleasing is Beauty, how sweet are the Charms!
How delightful Embraces, how peaceful her Arms!
Sure there's nothing so easy as learning to love;
'Tis taught us on Earth, and by all Things above:
And to Beauty's bright Standard all Heroes must yield,
For 'tis Beauty that conquers, and keeps the fair Field.

SONG XVIII.

See what a Conquest Love has made!
Beneath the Myrtle's am'rous Shade
The charming fair *Corinna* lies;
And, melting in Desire,
Quenching in Tears those flowing Eyes
That set the World on Fire.

What cannot Tears and Beauty do!
The Youth by chance stood by, and knew
For whom those Crystal Streams did flow;
And though he ne'er before
To her Eyes' brightest Rays did bow,
Weeps too, and does adore.

So when the Heav'ns, serene and clear,
Gilded with gaudy Light appear,
Each craggy Rock, and every Stone,
Their native Rigour keep;
But when in Rain the Clouds fall down,
The hardest Marbles weep.

SONG XIX.

Busk ye, busk ye, my bony Bride ;
Busk ye, busk ye, my bony Marrow ;
Busk ye, busk ye, my bony Bride,
Busk and go to the Braes of Yarrow ;
There we will sport and gather Dew,
Dancing while Lavrocks sing the Morning ;
There learn frae Turtles to prove true ;
O *Bell*, ne'er vex me with thy scorning.

To Westlin Breezes *Flora* yields,
And when the Beams are kindly warming,
Blythness appears o'er all the Fields,
And Nature looks mair fresh and charming.
Learn frae the Burns that trace the Mead,
Tho' on their Banks the Roses blossom,
Yet hastylie they flow to *Tweed*,
And pour their Sweetness in his Bosom.

Hast ye, hast, my bony *Bell*,
Hast to my Arms, and there I'll guard thee ;
With free Consent my Fears repel,
I'll with my Love and Care reward thee.
Thus sang I softly to my Fair,
Wha raised my Hopes with kind Relenting !
O Queen of Smiles, I ask nae mair,
Since now my bony *Bell's* consenting.

THE WHINING LOVER.

SONG I.

By a dismal Cypress lying,
Damon cry'd, all pale and dying,
Kind is Death, that ends my Pain,
But cruel She I loved in vain.

    The mossy Fountains
    Murmur my Trouble,
    And hollow Mountains
    My Groans redouble:
    Every Nymph mourns me,
    Thus while I languish;
    She only scorns me,
    Who caus'd my Anguish.

No Love returning me, but all Hope denying;
By a dismal Cypress lying,
Like a Swan so sung he dying:
Kind is Death, that ends my Pain,
But cruel She I lov'd in vain.

SONG II.

Go thou perpetual whining Lover,
For Shame leave off this humble Trade,
'Tis more than Time thou gav'st it over,
For Sighs and Tears will never move her;
By them more obstinate she's made,
And thou by Love, fond constant Love betray'd.

The more, vain Fop, thou su'st unto her,
The more she does **torment** thee still;
Is more perverse the more you wooe her,
When thou art humblest, lays thee lower;
And when most prostrate to her Will,
Thou meanly begg'st for Life, does basely kill.

By Heaven! 'tis against all Nature,
Honour and Manhood, Wit and Sense,
To let a little female Creature
Rule, on the poor Account of **Feature**;
And thy unmanly Patience
Monstrous and Shameful as her Insolence.

Thou may'st find **Forty will** be kinder,
Or more compassionate at least;
If one will serve **two** Hours will find her,
And half this Do **for** ever bind her
As firm and true as thy own Breast,
On Love and Virtue's double Interest.

But if thou can'st not live without her,
This only She, when it comes to 't,
And **she relent not** (as I doubt her),
Never make more ado about her.
To sigh and whimper is no Boot;
Go hang thy self, and that will do 't.

SONG III.

Sad *Philocles* sigh'd to the Wind,
The Wind it lamented his Moan,
Whilst Echo stood pining behind,
And gave him back every Groan.
Ye Winds! have the Grace to be mov'd,
Complaining, the fond Shepherd said,
The hard-hearted Nymph is reprov'd
By the gentle Returns ye have made.

To Echo himself he address'd;
Compassion, says he, thou hast shown,
Which proves, that the Pains of thy Breast
Are almost as great as my own.
'Twill yield me some little Relief,
With you a Companion to stray;
The Night shall be spent in my Grief,
In Tales of your Sorrow the Day.

The languishing Theme of your Woe,
The Shepherd Narcissus shall be;
For *Phillis* I'll mourn where I go,
Till grown a mere Shadow like thee.
Come, pitying Maid, let's retire,
To whisper our Plaints in a Cave:
The pitiful Nymph said Retire,
Such Places are likest the Grave.

At last, on the Side of a Hill,
A damp dusky Cavern they found:
There *Philocles* sigh'd to his fill,
And Echo repeated the Sound;
But yet the sad Nymph had an Art,
Whereby she would flatter his Pains;
Tho' speaking the Thoughts of her Heart,
She seem'd but repeating the Swain's.

He seated himself on the Ground,
His Hand it supported his Head;
Despairing he shew'd every Wound
The changing false *Phillis* had made:
If once on his Rival he thought,
Ye Gods! in a Rage he would cry,
Oh! blast all the Charms she has got,
For whom I thus languishing die.

Narcissus was still Echo's Thought;
Ye Gods! the sad Nymph would reply,
Oh! blast all the Charms he has got,
For whom I thus languishing die.
Thus *Philocles* dy'd in Despair,
While Echo augmented his Pain;
When dead, the sad Nymph did repair
To another sad desp'rate Swain.

SONG IV.

Help me, each harmonious Grove,
Gently whisper, all ye Trees,
Tune each warbling Throat to love,
And cool each Mead with softest Breeze.
Breath sweet Odour, ev'ry Flow'r,
All your various Paintings show;
Pleasing Verdure grace each Bow'r,
Around let ev'ry Blessing flow.

Glide ye limpid Brooks along,
Phaebus, glance thy mildest Ray;
Murmuring Floods, repeat my Song,
And tell what *Colin* dare not say.
Celia comes! whose charming Air
Fires with Love the rural Swains;
Tell, ah! tell the blooming Fair,
That *Colin* dies if she disdains.

SONG V.

I love, I doat, I rave with Pain,
No Quiet's in my Mind,
Tho' ne'er could be a happier Swain,
Were *Sylvia* less unkind;
For when (as long her Chains I've worn)
I ask Relief from Smart;
She only gives me Looks of Scorn;
Alas! 'twill break my Heart!

My Rivals rich in worldly Store,
May offer Heaps of Gold;
But surely I a Heav'n adore,
Too pretious to be sold.
Can *Sylvia* such a Coxcomb prize,
For Wealth and not Desert;
And my poor Sighs and Tears despise?
Alas, 'twill break my Heart!

When like some panting, hov'ring Dove,
I for my Bliss contend,
And plead the cause of eager Love,
She coldly calls me Friend.
Ah, *Sylvia!* thus in vain you strive
To act a Healer's Part;
'Twill keep but ling'ring Pain alive,
Alas! and break my Heart.

When on my lonely, pensive Bed,
I lay me down to rest,
In hopes to calm my raging Head,
And cool my burning Breast,
Her Cruelty all Ease denies;
With some sad Dream I start,
All drown'd in Tears I find my Eyes,
And breaking feel my Heart.

Then rising, thro' the Path I rove,
That leads me where she dwells,
Where to the senseless Walls my Love
Its mournful Story tells;
I view thy Window, kiss thy Door,
Till Morning bids depart,
Then vent ten thousand Sighs, and more;
Alas! 'twill break my Heart!

But, *Sylvia*, when this Conquest's won,
And I am dead and cold,
Renounce the cruel Deed you've done,
Nor glory when 'tis told;
For ev'ry lovely generous Maid
Will take my injur'd Part,
And curse thee *Sylvia*, I'm afraid,
For breaking my poor Heart.

SONG VI.

Come, all ye Youths, whose Hearts e'er bled
By cruel Beauty's Pride,
Bring each a Garland on his Head,
Let none his Sorrows hide;
But Hand in Hand around me move,
Singing the saddest Tales of Love;
And see, when your Complaints ye join,
If all your Wrongs can equal mine.

The happiest Mortal once was I,
My Heart no Sorrows knew;
Pity the Pain with which I die,
But ask not whence it grew.
Yet if a tempting Fair you find,
That's very lovely, very kind,
Tho' bright as Heaven, whose Stamp she bears,
Think of my Fate and shun her Snares.

SONG VII.

Like a wandering Ghost I appear,
All silent, neglected, and sad,
Tormented by Hopes and Despair,
I sigh when all others are glad.

No Joys in this Town can I find,
The City's a Desert to me;
I scarce shou'd regret being blind
To all other Objects but thee.

In the Fields as I saunter along,
I look but for thee in my Way;
And if from my Sight thou art gone,
I mourn all the rest of the Day:
Or if that by chance thou art there,
I shun every Mortal I meet,
Nor relish the Walk, or the Air;
Thou only can render them sweet.

O, *Nancy*, whilst thus I complain,
Does your Heart never flutter nor beat?
And have you no Sense of my Pain,
Whilst the Torment I bear is so great?
Must these wandering Eyes always rove
On every new Object you see?
Or must you reward my true Love,
And fix them at last upon me?

SONG VIII.

With broken Words, and down-cast Eyes,
Poor *Colin* spoke his Passion tender;
And parting with his *Grissy*, cries,
Ah! woe's my Heart that we should sunder!

To others I'm as cold as Snow,
But kindle with their Eyes like Tinder;
From thee with Pain I'm forc'd to go;
It breaks my Heart that we should sunder.

Chain'd to thy Charms, I cannot range,
No Beauty new my Love shall hinder;
Nor Time, nor Place shall ever change
My Vows, tho' we're oblig'd to sunder.

The Image of thy graceful Air,
And Beauties which excite our Wonder;
Thy lively Wit, and Prudence rare,
Shall still be present, tho' we sunder.

Dear Nymph, believe thy Swain in this,
You'll ne'er engage a Heart that's kinder;
Then seal a Promise with a Kiss,
Always to love me, tho' we sunder.

Ye Gods! take care of my dear Lass,
That as I leave her I may find her;
When that blest Time shall come to pass,
We'll meet again, and never sunder.

SONG IX.

Whilst I gaze on *Cloe*, trembling,
Straight her Eyes my Fate declare;
When she smiles, I fear dissembling;
When she frowns, I then despair.
Jealous of some rival Lover,
If a wand'ring Look she give;
Fain I would resolve to leave her,
But can sooner cease to live.

Why should I conceal my Passion,
Or the Torments I endure?
I'll disclose my Inclination,
Awful Distance yields no Cure.
Sure it is not in her Nature
To be cruel to her Slave;
She is too divine a Creature
To destroy what she can save.

Happy's he whose Inclination
Warms but with a gentle Heat,
Never mounts to raging Passion;
Love's a Torment, if too great:
When the Storm is once blown over,
Soon the Ocean quiet grows,
But a constant, faithful Lover,
Seldom meets with true Repose.

SONG X.

One Night, when all the Village slept,
Myrtillo's sad Despair
The wand'ring Shepherd waking kept,
To tell the Woods his Care:
Begone, said he, fond Thoughts, begone;
Eyes, give your Sorrows o'er:
Why shou'd you waste your Tears for one
That thinks on you no more?

Yet all the Birds, the Flocks, and Powers,
That dwell within this Grove,
Can tell how many tender Hours
We here have pass'd in Love:
The Stars above, my cruel Foes,
Have heard how she has sworn
A thousand times, that like to those
Her Flame shou'd ever burn.

But since she's lost, oh! let me have
My Wish, and quickly die.
In this cold Bank I'll make a Grave,
And there for ever lie.
Sad Nightingales the Watch shall keep,
And kindly here complain;
Then down the Shepherd lay to sleep,
And never wak'd again.

SONG XI.

As when on Mountain-heads,
With sudden Spring of Light,
The Sun his Splendor spreads,
And blinds the dazl'd Sight;
From *Mariana's* Eyes
Love throws a flashing Dart,
That wounds, with gay Surprize,
And festers in the Heart.

At dead of Night, when Care
Forsakes each tortured Breast,
I only, thro' Despair,
Am barr'd from gentle Rest.
When Morning Beams dispel
The gloomy Shades of Night,
Redoubled is my Hell,
While others reap Delight.

At Noon, when Day's enthron'd,
My Sorrows grow intense;
Nor is my Case bemoan'd
When silent Hours commence.
Then hasten, friendly Death,
And ease me from my Woe;
Who wou'd not yield his Breath,
When Love declar'd his Foe?

SONG XII.

Since from my dear *Astraea's* Sight
I was so rudely torn,
My Soul has never known Delight
Unless it was to mourn.

But oh, alas! with weeping Eyes
And bleeding Heart I lie;
Thinking on her, whose Absence 'tis
That makes me wish to die.

SONG XIII.

Beneath a gloomy Shade,
For unhappy Lovers made,
The poor despairing *Lycedas* was laid,
While drooping Turtles cooing stood
On the green Branches of the dusky Wood;
The mournful Flutes contend in vain
To lull his Cares, to ease his Pain;
His Pain and Cares thus force him to complain:
"Ah, heedless Shepherds! guard your Hearts
"From Woman's fatal Eyes;

"They wound us still with poison'd Darts,
"And he that's wounded dies:
"Their Form and Face, like Seas serene,
"Still promise only Joy;
"But oh! the Shelves, their Hearts within,
"Are certain to destroy.
"Ah! let my Fate thy Wreck prevent,
"Nor venture from the Shore."
But here the hapless Shepherd, spent
In Sighs, sunk down, and said no more.

SONG XIV.*

The Sun had just withdrawn his Fires,
And *Phaebus* shone with milder Ray,
When *Thyrsis* to the Grove retires,
As Love had pointed out the Way.

---

* By a printer's error, apparently, this song is numbered XVI. in the original, and the others numbered on from it. It seemed unnecessary, however, to perpetuate this error, so the printer has given it its proper number, and thus Songs XIV. to end of this book are numbered two lower than the corresponding songs in the original.

His trembling Knees the Turf receives,
His aching Head the Cowslips press:
His Breast, that Sighs alone had eas'd,
At last gave way to this Address:

O Queen, that guid'st the silent Hours,
If e'er *Endymion* sooth'd thy Pain,
By all thy Joys in *Carian* Bow'rs,
Restore me *Rosalind* again.

To thee my mournful Plaint I send,
Protectress of the virtuous Mind;
Do thou thy chaste Assistance lend,
Venus is leud and *Cupid* blind.

Behold these Cheeks, how pale, how wan,
That once were grac'd with rosie Pride:
Dim are my Eyes, their Lustre gone,
My Lips a purple Hue deride.

To wretched me it nought avails
That *Phaebus'* self has strung my Lyre,
Since *Plutus*, worthless God, prevails,
And only sordid Wealth can fire.

The Nightingale, that pines with Love,
With melting Notes does Grief suspend;
Me Verse, nor sweetest Sounds can move,
My Torments she alone can end.

But hark! the Raven's direful Croak,
Join'd with the Owl's ill-boding Shriek,
In frightful consort Fate here spoke;
Alas! my Love-sick Heart will break.

Too cruel Nymph, haste, haste away,
And see your Victim prostrate lye;
I faint, I can no longer stay,
O *Rosalind*, for thee I die!

SONG XV.

At length I feel the Power of Love
No more preserv'd by Reason's Arms;
Reason, alas! in vain does prove
Before *Maria's* killing Charms.

When first her Form, divinely fair,
Resistless struck my ravish'd Sight,
Not knowing there was Danger near,
I gaz'd with Wonder and Delight.

But O! too late, I found her Eyes
Could Pains, as well as Joys, impart;
From them a fatal Glance there flies
Which **pierces** me quite thro' the Heart.

Bright *Caelia's* Shape I have admir'd,
By blooming *Cloe's* Face been charm'd,
Aminta's poinant Wit has fir'd,
And *Daelia's* Voice my Breast has warm'd.

Each Female could Delight **inspire**,
To every Charm I us'd to bow;
But oh! tho' each cou'd raise Desire,
I **never, never** lov'd till now.

SONG XVI.

Was *Cloe* as kind as she's fair,
Good-natur'd, and witty, and free,
What Nymph could with *Cloe* compare,
Or Swain be as **happy as me?**

But oh! when I tell her of Love,
She seems not to know what I mean;
Cou'd she but my Passion approve,
How happy! how blest had I been!

Each Day my **Complaints** I renew,
I'languish, I pine, and I grieve;
In vain for Compassion I sue;
She neither will hear nor believe.

Gods! must I her Scorn then endure?
And **are** my fond Hopes all in vain?
Come, Death, then, and give me a Cure,
And **ease me** of *Celia's* Disdain.

THE SAUCY LOVER.

SONG I.

Of all Things beneath the Sun,
To love 's the greatest Curse;
If one's deny'd, then he's undone,
If not, 'tis ten times worse.
Poor *Adam* by his Wife, 'tis known,
Was trick'd some Years ago;
But *Adam* was not trick'd alone,
For all his Sons were so.

Lovers the strangest Fools are made,
When they their Nymphs pursue,
Which they will ne'er believe, till wed,
But then, alas! 'tis true.
They beg, they pray, and they adore,
'Till weary'd out of Life;
And pray, what's all this Trouble for?
Wy, truly, for a Wife.

How odd a Thing's a whining Sot,
Who sighs in greatest Need
For that, which soon as ever got,
Does make him sigh indeed.
Each Maid's an Angel whilst she's woo'd,
But when the Wooing's done,
The Wife, instead of Flesh and Blood,
Proves nothing but a Bone.

Ills, more or less, in human Life
No mortal Man can shun;
But when a Man has got a Wife,
He has them all in one.

The Liver of *Prometheus*
A growing Vulture fed;
A Fable that the Thing was thus,
The poor old Man was wed.

A Wife, all Men of Learning know,
Was *Tantalus's* Curse;
The Apples which did tempt him so,
Were nought but a Divorce.
Let no Fool dream that to his Share
A better Wife will fall;
They're all the same, faith, to a Hair,
For they are Women all.

When first the senseless empty Nokes
With Wooing does begin,
Far better he might beg the Stocks
That they would let him in.
Yet for a Lover we may say,
He wears no cheating Phiz;
Though other's Looks do oft betray,
He looks like what he is.

More Joys a Glass of Wine does give
(Wife take him that gainsays)
Than all the Wenches sprung from *Eve*
E'er gave in all their Days.
But come, to Lovers here's a Glass,
God-wot, they need no Curse;
Each wishes he may wed his Lass,
No Soul can wish him worse.

SONG II.

Woman, thoughtless, giddy Creature;
Laughing, idle, flutt'ring Thing!
Most fantastick Work of Nature!
Still like Fancy on the Wing.

Slave to ev'ry changing Passion,
Loving, hating, in extream:
Fond of every foolish Fashion;
And, at best, a pleasing Dream.

Lovely Trifle! dear Illusion!
Conqu'ring Weakness! wisht-for Pain!
Man's chief Glory, and Confusion,
Of all Vanities most vain!

Thus, deriding Beauty's Power,
Bevil call'd it all a Cheat;
But in less than half an Hour,
Kneel'd, and whin'd, at *Celia's* Feet.

SONG III.

Why so pale and wan, fond Lover?
Prithee why so pale?
Will, when looking well can't move her,
    Looking ill prevail?
      Prithee why so pale?

Why so dull and mute, young Sinner?
Prithee why so mute?
Will, when speaking well won't win her,
    Saying nothing do 't?
      Prithee why so mute?

Quit, quit for Shame this will not move,
This cannot take her;
If of herself she will not love,
    Nothing can make her:
      The Devil take her.

SONG IV.

As the Snow in Vallies lying,
Phaebus his warm Beams applying,
Soon dissolves and runs away;
So the Beauties, so the Graces,
Of the most bewitching Faces,
At approaching Age decay.

As a Tyrant, when degraded,
Is despis'd and is upbraided
By the Slaves he once controul'd,
So the Nymph, if none could move her,
Is contemn'd by every Lover
When her Charms are growing old.

Melancholy Looks, and Whining,
Grieving, Quarrelling, and Pining,
Are th' Effects your Rigours move;
Soft Caresses, amorous Glances,
Melting Sighs, transporting Trances,
Are the blest Effects of Love.

Fair ones, while your Beauty's blooming,
Imploy Time, lest Age resuming
What your Youth profusely lends,
You are robb'd of all your Glories,
And condemn'd to tell old Stories
To your unbelieving Friends.

SONG V.

Prithee *Billy*, ben't so silly
Thus to waste thy Days in Grief;
You say *Betty* will not let ye;
But can Sorrow bring Relief?

Leave repining, cease your whining,
Pox on Torment, Tears, and Woe;
If she's tender, she'll surrender,
If she's tough—e'en let her go.

SONG VI.

Why all this Whining?
Why all this Pining?
Love is a Folly, and Beauty is vain;
Nothing so common
As Wealth and Woman
To raise the Spirits and dull the Brain.

To him that's merry,
That's frolick and airy,
Nothing is grievous, nor nothing is sad;
Then rouse thy Spirit,
And take off thy Claret,
In one smiling Bumper a Cure's to be had.

If *Cloe* fly thee,
And still deny thee,
Never look sneaking, nor ever repine;
If 'tis her Fashion
To slight your Passion,
Then seem most easy, and deny her thine.

When next you meet her,
Again entreat her,
And if you find she wou'd make you her Tool,
Ne'er let it vex you,
Or once perplex you;
She'll soon repent it, and find who's the Fool.

SONG VII.

Lovers, who waste your Thoughts and Youth
In Passion's fond Extreams;
Who dream of Woman's Love and Truth,
And doat upon your Dreams.

I shou'd not here your Fancy take
From such a pleasing State,
Were you not sure at last to wake,
And find your Fault too late.

Then know, betimes, the Love which crowns
Our Cares is all but Wiles,
Compos'd of false fantastick Frowns,
And soft dissembling Smiles.

With Anger, which sometimes they feign,
They cruel Tyrants prove;
And then turn Flatterers again,
With as affected Love.

As if some Injury were meant
To whom they kindly us'd;
Those Lovers are the most content,
Who still have been refused.

Since in our Bosom each has nurst
A false and fawning Foe,
'Tis just, and wise, by striking first,
To 'scape the fatal Blow.

SONG VIII.

With Arts oft practis'd and admir'd,
A youthful Swain, by Love inspir'd,
Long Time pursu'd a Fair:
Her Coldness equal to his Love,
His Hopes repuls'd, his Fear improve,
And added to his Care.

With Sighs, and Tears, in vain he tries,
But deaf to all his Sighs, she flies,
As fast as he pursues;
To which he answers in Disdain,
By trying to augment my Pain,
Yourself the Conquest lose.

'Tis true I love you, cruel Maid,
But Love with Love must be repaid,
To make our Bliss compleat:
Since I've requested, you've deny'd,
My Love, as well as yours, is try'd;
And I with Ease retreat.

SONG IX.

What means this Niceness now of late,
Since Time that Truth does prove?
Such Distance may consist with State,
But never will with Love.
'Tis either Cunning or Disdain
That does such Ways allow;
The first is base, the last is vain;
May neither happen t' you.

For if it be to draw me on,
You over-act your Part;
And if it be to have me gone,
You need not half that Art;
For if you chance a Look to cast
That seems to be a Frown,
I'll give you all the Love that's past,
The rest shall be my own.

SONG X.

Never more I will protest
To love a Woman, but in jest;
For as they cannot be true,
So to give each Man his due,
When the Wooing Fit is past,
Their Affection cannot last.

Therefore if I chance to meet
With a Mistress fair and sweet,
She my Service shall obtain,
Loving her for Love again:
This much Liberty I crave,
Not to be a constant Slave.

For when we have try'd each other,
If she better like another,

Let her quickly change for me ;
Then to change am I as free.
He or she that loves too long,
Sells their Freedom for a Song.

SONG XI.

Still, *Cloe*, ply thy courtly Art,
Touch and retouch thy Face,
'Till the Cosmatick Powers impart
A Bloom to ev'ry Grace.

What though the home-bred country Maid,
To modest Rule's a Slave,
Disdains all use of White and Red,
But what plain Nature gave.

Yet if to vie with thee she dare,
Whoe'er the Umpire be,
He must be blind, or **must refer**
The Palm entire to thee.

For whilst her awkward Cheeks display
Pale Rage, or blushing Shame,
No Change thy steddy Looks betray,
They always shine the same.

SONG XII.

Belinda's Pride's an errant Cheat,
A foolish Artifice to blind ;
Some honest Glance, that scorn Deceit,
Does still reveal her native Mind.

With Look demure, and forc'd Disdain,
She idly acts the Saint ;
We see thro' this Disguise as plain
As we distinguish Paint.

The Pains she takes are vainly meant
To hide her am'rous Heart ;
'Tis like perfuming an ill Scent ;
The Smell's too strong for Art.

So have I seen grave Fools design,
With formal Looks to pass for Wise ;
But Nature is a Light will shine,
And break thro' all Disguise.

SONG XIII.

I'll tell you what, dear *Betty*:
I own you 'r wonderous pretty;
  I also confess
  Your elegant Dress,
And that you're passing witty.

But let not Vanity fool ye,
For I must tell you truly,
  I ne'er can abide
  To worship your Pride,
My Will is so unruly.

I'm not the Fool you'd have me;
No Tyrant can enslave me;
  No Prude alive
  Shall me deprive
Of the Liberty Nature gave me.

Tho' Beauty at first inclin'd me,
Good Humour alone can bind me;
  Then if you think fit
  Your Flouting to quit,
A Faithful Lover you'll find me.

SONG XIV.

Tho', *Flavia*, to my warm Desire
You mean no kind Return,
Yet still with undiminish'd Fire
You wish to see me burn.

Averse my Anguish to remove,
You think it wond'rous right
That I love on, for ever love,
And you for ever slight.

But you and I shall ne'er agree,
So gentle Nymph adieu;
Since you no Pleasure have for me,
I'll have no Pain for you.

SONG XV.

Sue to *Caelia* for the Favour,
Why shou'd poor deluded Man,

As if he were sole Receiver,
And return'd no Bliss again?

Were not Love condemn'd to Blindness,
Surely he wou'd quickly find,
Tho' to him she feigns the Kindness,
She is to herself most kind.

Let us banish then the Fashion,
And be resolutely brave;
Since it is their Inclination,
Let 'em ask before they have.

SONG XVI.

Fair *Iris* I love, and I hourly die,
But not for a Lip or a languishing Eye;
She's fickle and false, and thus we agree,
For I am as false and as fickle as she;
We neither believe what either can say,
And neither believing, we neither betray.

'Tis civil to hear, and say Things, of course;
We mean not the taking for better for worse;
When present we love, when absent agree,
I think not of *Iris*, nor *Iris* of me;
The Legend of Love no Couple can find
So easy to part, or so equally join'd.

SONG XVII.

Young *Cupid* one Day wily,
With well-dissembled Art;
Let fly an Arrow slily,
And pierced me to the Heart.

A while I sigh'd, grew stupid;
But to quit Scores with *Cupid*,
I found a Way, which soon I'll try,
Since Reason takes my Part.

I'll steal away his Arrows,
And sweet Revenge pursue;
With Women's Hearts I'll head 'em,
And then they'll ne'er fly true.

SONG XVIII.

The Mind of a Woman can never be known,
You never guess it aright:
I'll tell you the Reason—she knows not her own,
It changes too often ere Night.
'Twould puzzle *Apollo*
Her Whimsies to follow;
His Oracle wou'd be a Jest:
She'll frown when she's kind,
Then quickly you'll find
She'll change like the Wind;
And often abuses
The Man that she chuses;
And what she refuses
Likes best.

SONG XIX.

When I see the bright Nymph who my Heart does enthral;
When I view her soft Eyes, her languishing Air,
Her Merit so great, my own Merit so small,
It makes me adore, and it makes me despair.

But when I consider that she squanders on Fools
All those Treasures of Beauty with which she is stor'd,
My Fancy it damps, my Passion it cools,
And it makes me despise what before I ador'd.

Thus sometimes I despair, and sometimes I despise;
I love, and I hate, but I never esteem;
The Passion grows up, when I view her bright Eyes,
Which my Rivals destroy when I look upon them.

How wisely does Nature Things different unite;
In such odd Compositions our Safety is found;
As the Blood of the Scorpion is a Cure for the Bite,
So her Folly makes whole whom her Beauty does wound.

SONG XX.

Woman's like the flutt'ring Ocean;
Who her pathless Ways can find?
Every Blast directs her Motion;
Now she's angry, now she's kind.

What a Fool's the vent'rous Lover,
Whirl'd and toss'd by every Wind!
Can the Bark the Port recover,
When the silly Pilot's blind?

SONG XXI.

Silly **Swain**, give o'er thy Wooing,
Sighing, Gazing, Kissing, Cooing;
All is very foolish Doing.

All that follows after Kisses,
The very best, the Bliss of Blisses,
Is as dull a Joy as this is.

Prove the Nymph, and taste her Treasure;
Tell me then, when full of Pleasure,
What dull Thing thou canst discover
Duller than a happy Lover.

SONG XXII.

'Twas in this Shade,
While the Winds play'd,
And the Birds warbled under each Bough;
While Fountains flow
Murm'ring below,
In my Arms *Phillis* utter'd this Vow:

Swain, when I prove
False to thy Love,
All the wing'd Nation no more shall sing;
No Leaf shall shoot;
Winds shall be mute;
And not a Murmur heard in the Spring.

Thus did she swear;
Pleas'd did I hear:
But Words of Women, when they are kind,
Shou'd last for ever
Grav'd with a Feather,
In the loose Leaves, the Water, or Wind.

Sweet as the Rose,
White as the Snows,
Like 'em soon faded, sullied, is Woman;
Fair like the Moon,
Changing as soon;
Bright as the Sun, and as the Sun common.

Like the frail Flow'r,
(Child of an Hour)
Such are her Beauties, such are our Blisses;
Opening when blooming,
Gayly consuming,
Ev'ry Bee sucks 'em, ev'ry Wind kisses.

SONG XXIII.

How wretched is the Slave to Love,
Who can no real Pleasures prove,
For still they're mix'd with Pain:
When not obtain'd, restless is the Desire;
Enjoyment puts out all the Fire,
And shews the Love was vain.

It wanders to another soon,
Wanes and increases like the Moon,
And, like her, never rests;
Brings Tides of Pleasure now, and then of Tears,
Makes Ebbs and Floods of Joys and Cares,
In Lover's wav'ring Breasts.

But, spite of Love, I will be free,
And triumph in the Liberty
I without him enjoy:
I' th' worst of Prisons I'll my Body bind,
Rather than change my free-born Mind
For such a foolish Toy.

SONG XXIV.

No scornful Beauty e'er shall boast
She makes me love in vain;
That Man's a Fool, when once he's crost,
If e'er he loves again.
To pine or whine I never can,
Nor tell her I must die;
'Tis something so beneath a Man,
I cannot—no, not I.

SONG XXV.

In *Phillis* all vile Jilts are met,
Foolish, uncertain, false Coquette;

Love is her constant welcome Guest,
And still the newest pleases best.
Quickly she likes, then leaves as soon;
Her Life on Woman's a Lampoon.

Yet for the Plague of human Race,
This Devil has an Angel's Face;
Such Youth, such Sweetness in her Look,
Who can be Man, and not be took?
What former Love, what Wit, what Art,
Can save a poor inclining Heart?

In vain a thousand Times an Hour
Reason rebels against her Pow'r;
In vain I rail, I curse her Charms;
One Look my feeble Rage disarms;
There is Enchantment in her Eyes;
Who sees 'em can no more be wise.

SONG XXVI.

Ye little *Loves*, that round her wait
To bring me Tydings of my Fate;
As *Celia* on her Pillow lies,
Ah, gently whisper, *Strephon* dies.

If this will not her Pity move,
And the proud Fair disdains to love,
Smile, and say, 'tis all a Lie,
And haughty *Strephon* scorns to die.

SONG XXVII.

I'm not one of your Fops, who, to please a coy Lass,
Can lie whining and pining, and look like an Ass:
Life is dull without Love, and not worth the possessing,
But Fools make a Curse, what was meant for a Blessing.
While his Godship's not rude, I'll allow him my Breast;
But by *Jove*, out he goes, should he once break my Rest.
I can toy with a Girl for an Hour, to allay
The Fluster of Youth, or the Ferment of May;
But must beg her Excuse not to bear Pains or Anguish,
For that's not to love, by her leave, but to languish.

THE MERRY LOVER.

SONG I.

My *Jeany* and I have toil'd
The live-long Summer Day,
Till we amaist were spoil'd
At making of the Hay.
Her Kurchy was of Holland clear,
Ty'd on her bonny Brow;
I wisper'd something in her Ear—
But what's that to you?

Her Stockings were of Kersey green,
As tight as ony Silk;
O sic a Leg was never seen;
Her Skin was white as Milk:
Her Hair was black as ane could wish,
And sweet, sweet was her Mou;
O *Jeany* daintily can kiss—
But what's that to you?

The Rose and Lilly both combine
To make my *Jeany* Fair;
There is nae Bennison like mine,
I have amaist no Care:
Only I fear my *Jeany's* Face
May cause mae Men to rue,
And that may gar me say Alas!—
But what's that to you?

Conceal thy Beauties if thou can,
Hide that sweet Face of thine,
That I may only be the Man
Enjoys those Looks divine.

O do not prostitute, my dear,
Wonders to common view,
And I with faithful Heart shall swear
For ever to be true.

King Solomon had Wives enew,
And mony a Concubine,
But I enjoy a Bliss mair true;
His Joys were short of mine:
And *Jeany's* happier than they;
She seldom wants her Due;.
All Debts of Love to her I pay—
And what is that to you?

SONG II.

Young *Corydon* and *Phillis*
Sate in a lovely Grove,
Contriving Crowns of Lillies,
Repeating Tales of Love
And something else: but what I dare not name.

But as they were a-playing,
She ogled so the Swain,
It sav'd her plainly saying
Let's kiss to ease our Pain,
And something else, &c.

A thousand times he kissed her
Upon the flow'ry Green;
But as he further prest her,
A pretty Leg was seen, &c.

So many Beauties viewing,
His Ardor still encreas'd,
And greater Joys pursuing,
He wander'd o'er her Breast, &c.

A last Effort she trying
His Passion to withstand,
Cry'd (but 'twas faintly crying)
Pray take away your Hand.

Young *Corydon* grown bolder,
The Minutes would improve;
This is the Time, he told her,
To show how much I love.

The Nymph seem'd almost dying,
Dissolv'd in amorous Heat;
She kiss'd, and told him sighing,
My Dear, your Love is great.

But *Phillis* did recover
Much sooner than the Swain;
She blushing ask'd her Lover,
Shall we not kiss again, &c.

Thus Love his Revels keeping,
Till Nature's at a stand,
From Talk they fell to sleeping,
Holding each other's Hand, &c.

SONG III.

Be wary, my *Caelia*, when *Celadon* sues,
These Wits are the Bane of your Charms;
Beauty, play'd against Reason, will certainly lose,
Warring naked with Robbers in Arms.

Young *Damon*, despised for his Plainess of Parts,
Has Worth that a Woman should prize;
He'll run the Race *out*, tho' he heavily *starts*,
And distance the short-winded *Wise*.

Your Fool is a Saint in the Temple of Love,
And kneels all his Life there to pray;
Your Wit but looks in, and makes Haste to remove,
'Tis a Stage he but takes in his Way.

SONG IV.

Ah! bright *Belinda*, hither fly,
And such a Light discover,
As may the absent Sun supply,
And chear the drooping Lover.

Arise, my Day, with speed arise,
And all my Sorrows banish,
Before the Sun of thy bright Eyes
All gloomy Terrors vanish.

No longer let me sigh in vain,
And curse the hoarded Treasure;
Why should you love to give us Pain,
When you were made for Pleasure?

The petty Powers of Hell destroy;
To save's the Pride of Heaven:
To you the first, if you prove coy;
If kind, the last is given.

The Choice then sure's not hard to make
Betwixt a Good and Evil;
Which Title had you rather take,
My *Goddess*, or my *Devil?*

SONG V.

Pious *Selinda* goes to Pray'rs,
If I but ask the Favour;
And yet the tender Fool's in Tears,
When she believes I'll leave her.

Would I were free from this Restraint,
Or else had Hopes to win her;
Wou'd she could make of me a Saint,
Or I of her a Sinner.

SONG VI.

Yes, I could love, if I could find
A Mistress fitted to my Mind,
Whom neither Gold nor Pride could move,
To change her Virtue or her Love.

Loves to go neat, not to go fine;
Loves for myself, and not for mine
Not City proud, nor nicely Coy,
But full of Love, and full of Joy.

Not childish young, nor Beldame old;
Not firey hot, nor icy cold;
Not gravely wise to rule the State,
Nor foolish to be pointed at.

Not worldly rich, nor basely poor;
Not chaste, nor a reputed Whore:
If such a one you can discover,
Pray, Sir, intitle me her Lover.

SONG VII.

Bright *Cynthia's* Power divinely great,
What Heart is not obeying?
A thousand *Cupids* on her wait,
And in her Eyes are playing.

She seems the Queen of Love to reign;
For she alone dispenses
Such Sweets as best can entertain,
The Gust of all the Senses.

Her Face a charming Prospect brings,
Her Breath gives balmy Blisses;
I hear an Angel when she sings,
And taste of Heaven in Kisses.

Four Senses thus she feasts with Joy,
From Nature's richest Treasure;
Let me the other Sense employ,
And I shall die with Pleasure.

SONG VIII.

If *Phillis* denies me Relief,
If she's angry, I'll seek it in Wine;
Though she laughs at my amorous Grief,
At my Mirth why should she repine?

Brisk sparkling Champaign shall remove
All the Griefs my dull Soul has in store:
My Reason I lost when I lov'd,
By drinking what can I do more?

Would *Phillis* but pity my Pain,
Or my amorous Vows would approve,
The Juice of the Grape I'd disdain,
And be drunk with nothing but Love.

SONG IX.

Three Nymphs contending for my Heart,
With different Charms and Grace;
The first sold Puddings, Pies, and Tarts;
The second, Pins and Lace;
The third employ'd herself to cry
The News three Times a Week,
Besides ev'ry Night 'twas her Delight
To cry hot baked Ox-cheek.

Look, Gods, from your Celestial Bow'rs,
And guide me to the best ;
And may my Faculties and Pow'rs
Of Heart and Mind be blest.

Whilst thus I cry'd, the Gods **reply'd**,
Thy Fate can't be revers'd ;
The Nymph we've chosen for thy **Bride**,
Sifts Cinders from the Dust.

SONG X.

Let us drink, and be merry,
Dance, joke, and rejoice,
With Claret and Sherry,
Theorbo and Voice.
The changeable World
To our Joy is unjust ;
All Treasure's uncertain,
The Down with your Dust.
In Frolicks dispose
Your Pounds, Shillings, and Pence,
For we shall be nothing
An hundred Years hence.
We'll kiss, and be free,
With *Moll*, *Betty*, and *Nelly* ;
Have Oysters, and Lobsters,
And Maids by the Belly.
Fish Dinners will make
A Lass spring like a Flea ;
Dame *Venus* (Love's Goddess)
Was born of the Sea :
With Bacchus, and with her
We'll tickle the Sense,
For we shall be past it
An hundred Years hence.
Your most beautiful **Bit**,
That hath all Eyes upon her,
That her Honesty sells
For a *Hatgoust* of Honour !
Whose Lightness and Brightness
Doth shine in such Splendour,
That none but the Stars
Are thought fit to attend her :

Though **now** she be pleasant,
And sweet to the Sense,
Will be damnably mouldy
An hundred Years hence.

SONG XI.

A certain Presbyterian Pair
Were wedded t' other Day,
And when in Bed the Lambs were laid,
Their Pastor came to pray.

But first he bade each Guest depart,
Nor sacred Rites prophane;
For carnal Eyes such Misteries
Can **never** entertain.

Then with a Puritanick Air,
Unto the Lord he pray'd;
That he would please to grant Encrease
To that same Man and Maid.

And that the Husbandman might dress
Full well the Vine, his Wife;
And like a Vine, she still might **twine**
About him all her Life.

Sack-posset then **he** gave them both,
And said with lifted Eyes,
Blest of the Lord! with one accord
Begin your Enterprize.

The Bridegroom then drew near his Spouse,
T' apply prolifick Balm;
And while they strove in mutual Love,
The Parson sung a Psalm.

SONG XII.

Caelia, too late you wou'd repent:
The offering all your Store
Is now but like a Pardon sent
To one that's dead before.

Your Bounty of those Favours shown,
Whose Worth you first deface,
Is melting valu'd Medals down,
And giving us the Brass.

O! since the Thing we beg's a Toy,
That's priz'd by Love alone,
Why cannot Women grant the Joy
Before the Love is gone.

SONG XIII.

Prithee, *Susan*, what dost muse on,
By this doleful Spring?
You are I fear in Love, my Dear;—
Alas, poor Thing!

SUSAN.

Truly, *Jamie*, I must blame ye,
You look so pale and wan;
I fear 'twill prove, you are in Love—
Alas, poor Man!

JAMES.

Nay, my *Suey*, now I view ye,
Well I know your Smart;
When you're alone, you sigh and groan—
Alas, poor Heart!

SUSAN.

Jamie, hold, I dare be bold
To say thy Heart is stole,
And know the She, as well as thee—
Alas, poor Soul!

JAMIE.

Then, my *Sue*, tell me who,
I'll give the Beads of Pearl,
And ease thy Heart of all this Smart—
Alas, poor Girl!

SUSAN.

Jamie, no; if you should know,
I fear 'twou'd make ye sad,
And pine away both Night and Day—
Alas, poor Lad!

JAMES.

Then, my *Sue*, it is for you
That I burn in these Flames;
And when I die, I know you'll cry,
Alas, poor *James*!

SUSAN.

Say you so, then *Jamie* know,
If you should prove untrue,
Then must I likewise cry,
Alas, poor *Sue!*

Quoth he, Then join thy Hand with mine,
And we will wed to Day.
I do agree, here 'tis, quoth she,
Come, let's away.

SONG XIV.

Do not ask me, charming *Phillis*,
Why I lead you here alone,
By this Bank of Pinks and Lillies,
And of Roses newly blown.

'Tis not to behold the Beauty
Of the Flowers that crown the Spring;
'Tis to——; but I know my Duty,
And dare never name the Thing.

What the Sun does to the Roses
When his Beams play sweetly in,
I wou'd——; but my Fear opposes,
And I dare not name the Thing.

On this Bank of Pinks and Lillies
Might I speak what I wou'd do,
I wou'd—— with my lovely *Phillis*,
I wou'd——, I wou'd——. Ah! wou'd you!

SONG XV.

O! I love a charming Creature,
But the Flame with which I burn
Is not for each tender Feature,
Nor for her Wit, nor sprightly Turn;
But for her down, down, derry down;
But for her down, down, derry down.

On the Grass I saw her lying;
Strait I seiz'd her tender Waste;
On her Back she lay complying,
With her lovely Body plac'd
Under my down, down, &c.

But the Nymph being young and tender,
Cou'd not bear the dreadful Smart;
Still unwilling to surrender,
Call'd Mamma to take the Part
Of her down, down, &c.

Out of Breath Mamma came running
To prevent poor *Nanny's* Fate;
But the Girl, now grown more cunning,
Cry'd, Mamma you're come too late;
For I am down, down, &c.

SONG XVI.

Come, be free, my lovely Lasses,
Banish dull restraining Pride;
Now we're o'er our generous Glasses,
Let the Mask be thrown aside.

With our Wine sweet Kisses blending,
You its Virtues shall improve;
Wine our warm Desires befriending,
Shall increase the Power of Love.

Squeamish Prudes may take Occasion,
Whilst they burn with inward Fire,
To condemn a generous Passion,
Which they never could inspire.

But how curs'd is their Condition,
Whilst in us they Freedom blame?
Every Night pant for Fruition,
Yet find none to meet their Flame.

SONG XVII.

Yes, all the World will sure agree,
He who's secure of having thee
Will be entirely blest;
But 'twere in me too great a Wrong
To make one who has been so long
My *Queen,* my *Slave* at last.

Nor ought these Things to be confin'd
That were for public Good design'd:
Could we in foolish Pride
Make the Sun always with us stay,
'Twould burn our Corn and Grass away,
And starve the World beside.

Let not the Thoughts of parting fright
Two Souls which Passion does unite;
For while our Love does last,
Neither will strive to go away;
And why the Devil shou'd we stay
When once that Love is past.

SONG XVIII.

Whenever, *Cloe*, I begin
Your Heart, like mine, to move,
You tell me of the crying Sin
Of unchaste lawless Love.

How can that Passion be a Sin
Which gave to *Cloe* Birth?
How can those Joys but be divine
Which make a Heav'n on Earth?

To wed, Mankind the Priests trepann'd
By some sly Fallacy,
And disobey'd God's great Command,
Increase and multiply.

You say that Love's a Crime, Content;
Yet this allow you must,
More Joy's in Heav'n when one repent,
Than over ninety Just.

Since then, dear Girl, for Heav'n's sake,
Repent, and be forgiv'n;
Bless me, and by Repentance make
A Holliday in Heav'n.

SONG XIX.

Peggy, in Devotion
Bred from tender Years,
From my loving Motion
Still was called to Pray'rs.

I made muckle Bustle
Love's dear Fort to win;
But the Kirk Apostle
Told her 'twas a Sin.

Fasting and Repentance,
And such whining Cant,
With the Doomsday Sentence,
Frighted my young Saint.

He taught her the Duty
Heavenly Joys to know;
I who lik'd her Beauty,
Taught her those below.

Nature took my Part still,
Sense did Reason blind,
That for all his Art, still
She to me inclin'd.

Strange Delights hereafter
Did so dull appear,
She, as I had taught her,
Vow'd to share 'em here.

Faith, 'tis worth your Laughter;
'Mongst the Canting Race,
Neither Son nor Daughter
Ever yet had Grace.

Peggy, on the *Sunday*,
With her Daddy vext,
Came to me on *Monday*,
And forgot his Text.

SONG XX.

Phillis, as her Wine she sipp'd in,
Gaily talking with her Swain,
Into her Hand he slily slipped in—
   Tal, lal, lal, lal—
A full Glass of brisk Champaigne.

Why so coy, said he, and fickle?
Must I always sigh in vain?
Must I never hope to tickle—
   Tal, lal, &c.—
Your Ear with a merry Strain?

Long have I been toss'd and fretting
Like a Sailor on the Main;
Sure, at length, 'tis Time to get in—
   Tal, &c.—
To the Port I hope to gain.

Hearts you take Delight in stealing,
Of new Conquest still are vain;
Torture others, whilst I'm feeling—
  Tal, &c.—
Pleasure that is void of Pain.

Won, at length, she listen'd kindly,
And from Love could not refrain;
So in the Nick the Nymph was finely—
  Tal, &c.—
Fitted for her cold Disdain.

SONG XXI.

'Twas Fancy first made *Celia* fair;
'Twas Fancy gave her Shape and Air;
It robb'd the Sun, stript every Star
Of Beauties to bestow on her;
And when it had the Goddess made,
Down it fell and worshiped.
Creator first, and then a Creature;
Narcissus and a Pail of Water.

SONG XXII.

Amongst the Willows on the Grass,
Where Nymphs and Shepherds lie,
Young *Willy* courted bonny *Bess,*
And *Nell* stood list'ning by:
Says *Will,* we will not tarry
Two Months before we marry.
No, no, fie no, never, never tell me so,
For a Maid I'll live and die.
Says Nell, *So shall not I,*
Says Nell, &c.

Long Time betwixt Hope and Despair,
And Kisses mixt between,
He with a Song did charm her Ear,
Thinking she chang'd had been;
Says *Will,* I want a Blessing
Substantialer than Kissing.
No, no, fie no, never, never tell me so,
For I will never change my Mind.
Says Nell, *She'll prove more kind,*
Says Nell, &c.

Smart Pain the Virgin finds,
Altho' by Nature taught
When she first to Man inclines:
Quoth Nell, *I'll venture that.*

Oh! who wou'd lose a **Treasure**
For such a puny Pleasure!
Not I, not I, no, a Maid I'll live and die,
And to my Vow be true.
Quoth Nell, *The more Fool you,*
Quoth Nell, &c.

To my Closet I'll repair,
And read on godly Books,
Forget vain Love, and Worldly Care.
Quoth Nell, *That likely looks.*

You Men are all perfidious,
But I will be religious;
Try all, fly all, and while I breathe, defy all;
Your Sex I now despise.
Says Nell, *By* Jove, *she lies.*
Says Nell, &c.

SONG XXIII.

If the Heart of a Man is depress'd with Cares,
The Mist is dispell'd when a Woman appears;
Like the Notes of a Fiddle, she sweetly, sweetly
Raises our Spirits, and charms our Ears.
Roses and Lillies her Cheek disclose,
But her ripe Lips are more sweet than those.
   Press her,
   Caress her,
   With Blisses
   Her Kisses
Dissolve us in Pleasure, and soft Repose.

SONG XXIV.

When I court thee, dear *Molly*, to grant me the Bliss,
With a squeeze by the Hand, and then with a Kiss,
You, like an arch Baggage, for ever reply,
In the same loving Mood, Can you live, Sir, and die?
Then you ask me, how long this same Passion will last,
And if I shan't cool when the Moment is past?

Such Questions as these might e'en damp a Beginner,
And must certainly puzzle an old batter'd Sinner.
But to show you, for once, how much I despise
To tell you, like some Men, a thousand damn'd Lyes,
My Mind, dearest Girl, in few Words you shall know,
And if, on those Terms, you think well of it, so;
If not, for my Part, I shall ne'er take it ill,
For if one Woman won't, there are thousands that will.

That I like you at present, you never can doubt;
For what do I take all this Trouble about?
That my Passion is real, and void of Disguise,
You may feel by my Pulse, you may read in my Eyes;
When these roll so fast, and that beats so quick,
The *deuce* must be in't if it's all but a Trick.

Thy fresh ruddy Lips, and thy Teeth all so white;
Thy round tempting Bubbies, which heave with Delight;
Thy trim taper Shape, and thy dear little Feet;
Thy Voice that's so soft, and thy Breath that's so sweet;
Thy bright beaming Eyes, and thy gay golden Hair,
Provoke a Sensation too killing to bear;
Above or below nothing faulty is seen;
And, faith, I dare answer for what lies between.

So many rare Charms surely never can cloy,
But Night after Night wou'd afford one new Joy;
Methinks in my Passion I never cou'd vary,
If a thousand Examples didn't prove the Contrary;
For, like other Men, I am but Flesh and Blood;
Yet, if I'm no better, I hope I'm as good:
Then since, dearest *Molly*, any one whom you take
Is as likely as me to prove false and forsake,
If you e'er run the Hazard, let me be your Man,
And I'll love you as much, and as long as I can.
We'll toy, romp, and revel, we'll bill and we'll coo,
And do everything else which young Lovers do.
But if, upon Tryal, and often repenting,
(For the Proof of the Pudding's, you know, in the eating)
Your Passion or mine from the Bias shou'd run,
As in Crowds of each Sex it already has done;
Shou'd we grow Cool and Civil, why e'en let us part,
Nor strive to keep up a dull Passion by Art;
For 'tis Folly, 'tis Nonsense, our Nature to force,
As spurring a Jade only makes her the worse:
At formal Restraint let us neither repine,
But give back my Heart, and I'll return thine.

SONG XXV.

Ye Nymphs, no more take Pains to hide
Your Love, but own your Passion;
For Virtue, if too nice, is Pride,
And Coyness Affectation.

Cupid makes you Virgins tender;
Make 'em easy to be won;
Let 'em presently surrender,
When the Treaty's once begun.

Such as like a tedious Wooing,
Let 'em cruel Damsels find;
But for such as wou'd be doing,
Prithee, *Cupid*, make 'em kind.

SONG XXVI.

My Name is honest *Harry*,
And I love little *Mary;*
In spite of *Ciss* or jealous *Bess*,
I'll have my own Fegary.

My Love is blithe and bucksome,
And sweet and fine as can be;
Fresh and gay as the Flow'rs in *May*,
And looks like *Jack-a-Dandy*.

And if she will not have me,
That am so true a Lover,
I'll drink my Wine, and ne'er repine,
And down the Stairs I'll shove her.

But if that she will love, Sir,
I'll be as kind as may be;
I'll give her Rings, and pretty Things,
And deck her like a Lady:

Her Petticoat of Satten,
Her Gown of Crimson Tabby,
Lac'd up before, and spangl'd o'er
Just like a Barthol'mew Baby.

Her Wastcoat shall be Scarlet,
With Ribbands ty'd together;
Her Stockings of a cloudy Blue,
And her Shoes of Spanish Leather;

Her Smock of finest Holland,
And lac'd in every Quarter,
Side and wide, and long enough
To hang below her Garter.

Then to the Church I'll have her,
Where we will wed together,
And so come Home when we have done,
In spite of Wind and Weather.

The Fiddlers shall attend us,
And first play *John come kiss me;*
And when that we have danc'd around,
Then strike up *Hit or miss me.*

Then hey for little *Mary,*
'Tis she I love alone, Sir :
Let any Man do what he can,
I will have her, or none, Sir.

SONG XXVII.

Tell me no more I am deceiv'd,
That *Cloe's* false and common ;
By Heav'n, I all along believ'd
She was a very Woman :
As such I lik'd, as such caress'd ;
She still was constant when possess'd :
She could do more for no Man.

But oh! her Thoughts on others ran ;
And that you think a hard Thing :
Perhaps she fancy'd you the Man ;
Why, what care I one Farthing!
You think she's false, I am sure she's kind ;
I'll take her Body, you her Mind :
Who has the better Bargain?

SONG XXVIII.

After the Pangs of a desperate Lover,
When Day and Night I have sigh'd all in vain,
Ah! what a Pleasure it is to discover
In her Eyes Pity who causes my Pain!
Ah! what a Pleasure it is to discover
In her Eyes Pity who causes my Pain!

When with Unkindness our Love at a Stand is,
And both have punish't ourselves with the Pain,
Ah! what a Pleasure the Touch of her Hand is!
Ah! what a Pleasure to press it again!

When the Denial comes fainter and fainter,
And her Eyes give what her Tongue does deny,
Ah! what a Trembling does usher my Joy!
Ah! what a Trembling, &c.

When with a Sigh she accords me the Blessing,
And her Eyes twinkle 'twixt Pleasure and Pain,
Ah! what a Joy 'tis, beyond all expressing!
Ah! what a Joy to hear, Shall we again?
Ah! what a Joy, &c.

SONG XXIX.

Young *Cupid* I find
To subdue me inclin'd,
But at length I a Stratagem found
That will rid me of him;
For I'll drink to the Brim,
And unless he can Swim,
He like other blind Puppies shall drown.

SONG XXX.

Dorinda has such pow'rful Arts,
Such an attractive Air,
None can resist her conqu'ring Darts,
But gladly yield their captive Hearts
To so divine a Fair.

Thus the mysterious Loadstone's Pow'r
Each wand'ring Atom draws;
From Pole to Pole they take their Course,
Confin'd by an intrinsick Force,
And Circle in its Laws.

Magnetick Pow'rs her Charm attend;
But then, here lies the Riddle:
The Loadstone does its Force extend,
And strongest draws at either End,
Dorinda in the Middle.

SONG XXXI.

Of *Anna's* Charms let others tell,
Or bright *Eliza's* Beauty;
My Song shall be of *Bouzabel*,
To sing of her's my Duty.
The Fair who armed with *Cupid's* Darts,
His Flames and other Matters,
Is all around behung with Hearts,
As Beggars are with Tatters.

To lavish Nature much she owes,
And much to Education;
The Girls and Boys, and Belles and Beaus,
Are struck with Admiration;
For blended in her Cheek there lies
The Carrot and the Turnip;
And who beholds her blazing Eyes,
His very Heart they burn up.

Her dainty Hands are red and blue;
Her Teeth all black and yellow;
Her curling Hair of saffron Hue;
Her Lips like any Tallow:
Her Voice so loud, and eke so shrill,
Far off it is admir'd;
Her Tongue, which never yet lay still,
And yet was never tir'd.

Ten thousand Wonders rise to View
All o'er the lovely Creature;
The pearly Sweat, like Morning Dew,
Gilds every shining Feature.
As *Isaac* of his *Esau* said,
She like a Forest savours:
Thrice happy Man! for whom the Maid
Reserves her hidden Favours.

O *Bouzabel*, for thee we pant,
To thee our Hopes aspire;
For thou has all which Lovers want
To quench their raging Fire.
Then kindly take us to thy Arms,
And in Compassion save us
From *Anna's* and *Eliza's* Charms,
Which cruelly enslave us.

SONG XXXII.

What tho' you cannot move her
With all your Art and Pressing?
Vex not, fond, silly Lover,
Nor curse the vain Addressing;
    Why shou'd you lament,
    When she shou'd repent?
What Help, if a Fool will deny thee?
    'Tis all but a miss
    Of a Face and a Kiss;
And there's a good Sex to supply thee.

Who knows, wou'd you but leave her,
What Change she may discover?
Perhaps may grant the Favour,
Rather than lose the Lover.
    If nothing avail,
    Yet, 'tis Odds if she fail
To give thee full Right to disdain her;
    When, after thy Love
    And thy Worth cou'd not move,
A Fool that has neither shall gain her.

Make Love an easy Fashion,
And thy Success thy Measure;
Discarding still the Passion
That will not bring the Pleasure.
    Examine not why
    The Lady is shy,
If Nature, or Honour advise her;
    But, thy Part fairly done,
    If she'll not be won,
Take Leave, and look out for a Wiser.

SONG XXXIII.

Love is now become a Trade;
All its Joys are bought and sold;
Money is a Feature made,
And Beauty is confin'd to Gold.

Courtship is but Terms of Art;
Portion, Settlement, and Dower
Soften the most obdurate Heart;
The Lawyer only is the Wooer.

My Stock can never reach a Wife;
It may a small retailing Whore:
Let Men of Fortune buy for Life,
A Night's a Purchase for the Poor.

SONG XXXIV.

'Tho' Women, 'tis true, are but tender,
Yet Nature does Strength supply:
Their Will is too strong to surrender,
They're obstinate still till they die.

In vain you attack 'em with Reason,
Your Sorrows you only prolong;
Disputing is always High Treason,
No Woman was e'er in the Wrong.
Your only Relief is to bear;
And when you appear content,
Perhaps, in Compassion, the Fair
May persuade herself into Consent.

SONG XXXV.

If you sue to *Venalia* to grant you the Blessing,
Like *Jove*, in Gold court her, or vain's your Addressing;
For she says that Love nought but what's gen'rous inspires,
And therefore rich Tokens of Love she requires.

Such Suitors as nothing but Love have to give her,
(Like pennyless Ghosts at the *Stygian* River,
To *Elysium* a Passage deny'd by old *Charon*)
Eternal Attendance may dance on the Fair one.

SONG XXXVI.

Cloe's a Goddess in the Groves,
A Naiad in the Streams;
An Angel in the Church she moves;
A Woman in my Dreams.

Love steals Artill'ry from her Eyes,
The Graces point her Charms;
Orpheus is rival'd in her Voice,
And *Venus* in her Arms.

Never so happily in one,
Did Heav'n and Earth combine;
And yet 'tis Flesh and Blood alone
Make her this Thing divine.

She looks like other Mortal Dames,
Till I unlace her Boddice;
But when with Fire she meets my Flames,
The Wench turns up a Goddess.

SONG XXXVII.

Sylvia the Fair, in the Bloom of fifteen,
Felt an innocent Warmth, as she lay on the Green:
She had heard of a Pleasure, and something she guest
By the towzing and tumbling and touching her Breast.
She saw the Men eager, but was at a Loss
What they meant by their Sighing, and Kissing so close;
  By their Praying and Whining,
  And Clasping and Twining,
  And Panting and Wishing,
  And Sighing and Kissing,
  And Sighing and Kissing so close.

Ah! she cry'd; ah for a languishing Maid
In a Country of Christians to die without Aid!
Not a Whig, or a Tory, or Trimmer at least,
Or a Protestant Parson, or Catholick Priest,
To instruct a young Virgin, that is at a Loss
What they meant by their Sighing and Kissing so close;
  By their Praying and Whining,
  And Clasping and Twining,
  And Panting and Wishing,
  And Sighing and Kissing,
  And Sighing and Kissing so close.

Cupid in Shape of a Swain did appear;
He saw the sad Wound, and in Pity drew near;
Then shew'd her his Arrow, and bid her not fear,
For the Pain was no more than a Maiden may bear.
When the Balm was infus'd she was not at a Loss
What they meant by their Sighing and Kissing so close;
  By their Praying and Whining,
  And Clasping and Twining,
  And Panting and Wishing,
  And Sighing and Kissing,
  And Sighing and Kissing so close.

SONG XXXVIII.

As naked almost, and more fair you appear
Than *Diana*, when spy'd by *Actaeon*;
Yet that Stag-hunter's Fate, your Votaries here,
We hope you're too gentle to lay on.

For he, like a Fool, took a Peep and no more,
So she gave him a large Pair of Horns, Sir:
What Goddess, undrest, such Neglect ever bore?
Or what Woman e'er pardon'd such Scorns, Sir?

The Man who with Beauty feasts only his Eyes,
With the Fair always works his own Ruin;
You shall find by your Actions, one Looks and one Sighs,
We're not barely contented with Viewing.

SONG XXXIX.

Since you will needs my Heart possess,
'Tis just to you I first confess
The Faults to which 'tis given:
It is to Change much more inclin'd
Than Woman, or the Sea or Wind,
Or aught that's under Heaven.

Nor will I hide from you this Truth,
It has been from its very Youth
A most egregious Ranger:
And since from me 't has often fled,
With whom it was both born and bred,
'Twill scarce stay with a Stranger.

The Black, the Fair, the Grey, the Sad,
(Which often made me fear 'twas mad)
With one kind Look cou'd win it;
So nat'rally it loves to range,
That it has left Success for Change,
And, what's worse, glories in it.

Oft, when I have been laid to Rest,
'Twould make me act like one possest,
For still 'twill keep a Pother;
And tho' you only I esteem,
Yet it will make me in a Dream
Court and enjoy Another.

And now, if you are not afraid,
After these Truths that I have said,
To take this arrant Rover;
Be not displeas'd, if I protest,
I think the Heart within your Breast
Will prove just such another.

SONG XL.

Would you have a young Virgin of fifteen Years,
You must tickle her Fancy with Sweets and Dress;
Ever toying and playing, and sweetly, sweetly
Sing a Love Sonnet, and charm her Ears;
Wittily, prettily talk her down;
Chuse her, and praise her, if fair or brown;
    Sooth her and smooth her,
    And teaze her and please her,
And touch but her Smisker, and all's your own.

Do you fancy a Widow well known in Man,
With a Front of Assurance come boldly on;
Be at her each Moment, and briskly, briskly
Put her in Mind how her Time steals on;
Rattle and prattle, altho' she frown;
Rouze her and touze her from Morn to Noon,
    And shew her some Hour
    You'll answer her Dow'r,
And get but her Writings, and all's your own.

Do you fancy a Punk of Humour free,
That's kept by a Fumbler of Quality,
You must rail at her Keeper, and tell her, tell her
That Pleasure's best Charm is Variety:
Swear her much fairer than all the Town;
Try her and ply her when *Cully's* gone;
    Dog her and jog her,
    And meet her and treat her,
And kiss with a Guinea, and all's your own.

THE PRESSING LOVER.

SONG I.

O *Bell*, thy Looks have kill'd my Heart,
I pass the Day with Pain;
When Night returns, I feel the Smart,
And wish for thee in vain.

I'm starving cold, while thou art warm;
Have Pity and incline,
And grant me for a Hap that charm-
-ing Petticoat of thine.

My ravisht Fancy, in amaze,
Still wanders o'er thy Charms;
Delusive Dreams ten thousand Ways
Present thee to my Arms:

But waking, think what I endure,
While cruel you decline
Those Pleasures, which can only cure
This panting Breast of mine.

I faint, I fail, I wildly rove,
Because you still deny
The just Reward that's due to Love,
And let true Passion die.

O turn, and let soft Pity seize
That lovely Breast of thine;
Thy Petticoat could give me Ease
If thou and it were mine.

Sure Heaven has fitted for Delight
That beauteous Form of thine;
And thou'rt too good its Law to slight
By hind'ring the Design.

May all the Powers of Love agree
At length to make thee mine;
Or loose my Chains, and set me free
From every Charm of thine.

SONG II.

Prithee, *Cloe* give o'er,
And perplex me no more,
For, my Charmer, it looks very queerly
That in blooming fifteen,
Thou'rt afraid to be seen
By a Shepherd who loves thee so dearly.

When with Speed I pursue,
Intending to Wooe,
And tell thee how much I'm thy Lover,
Like a fearful young Lamb,
That runs after its Dam,
So thou flyest away to thy Mother.

I know't has been told,
That Patriarchs of old
Spent threescore years in their Wooing;
'Twas no Wonder, then,
That a Nymph of Fifteen
Should be coy when a Swain was pursuing.

But, my Charmer, I vow,
'Tis a Miracle now,
That a Nymph in her Teens should fly any,
When I dare now engage
Not a Man in the Age
But thinks Threescore Days are too many.

SONG III.

Fye *Liza*, scorn the little Arts
Which meaner Beauties use,
Who think they ne'er secure our Hearts
Unless they still refuse;
Are coy and shy; will seem to frown,
To raise our Passion higher;
But when the poor Delight is known,
It quickly palls Desire.

Come, let's not trifle Time away,
Or stop you know not why;
Your Blushes and your Eyes betray
What Death you mean to die;
Let all your Maiden Fears begone,
And Love no more be crost:
Ah! *Liza*, when the Joys are known
You'll curse the Minutes past.

SONG IV.

A Nymph of the Plain,
By a jolly young Swain,
By a jolly young Swain
Was addressed to be kind:
But relentless I find
To his Pray'rs she appear'd,
Tho' himself he endear'd,
In a manner so soft, so engaging and sweet,
As soon might persuade her his Passion to meet.

How much he ador'd her,
How oft he implor'd her,
How oft he implor'd her
I cannot express;
But he lov'd to Excess,
And swore he wou'd die
If she wou'd not comply,
In a manner, &c.

While Blushes, like Roses,
Which Nature composes,
Which Nature composes,
Vermillioned her Face
With a beautiful Grace,
Which her Lover improv'd
When he found he had mov'd,
In a manner, &c.

When wak'd from the Joy
Which their Souls did employ,
From her ruby warm Lips
Thousand Odours he sips;
At the Sight of her Eyes
He faints and he dies,
In a manner, &c.

But how they shall part
Now becomes all the Smart,
Now becomes all the Smart;
Till he vow'd to his Fair,
That to ease his own Care
He would meet her again,
And till then be in Pain,
In a manner so soft, so engaging and sweet,
As soon might persuade her his Passion to meet.

SONG V.

Caelia, let not Pride undo you,
Love and Life fly swiftly on;
Let not *Damon* still pursue you,
Still in vain till Love is gone:
See how fair the blooming Rose is,
See by all how justly priz'd;
But when it its Beauty loses,
See the wither'd Thing despised.

When these Charms that Youth have lent you
Like the Roses are decay'd,
Caelia, you'll too late repent you,
And be forc'd to die a Maid.
Die a Maid! die a Maid! die a Maid!
Caelia, you'll too late repent you,
And be forced to die a Maid.

SONG VI.

Caelia, my dearest, no longer depress me,
But hasten to bless me,
And fly to my Arms.
O cou'd I charm you!
How I wou'd warm you!
How I wou'd revel and sport in your Arms!

No one is near;
Why should we fear?
Why should we these pretious Moments delay?
If I've offended,
I ne'er intended;
I'll beg your Pardon another Day.

SONG VII.

By the Mole on your Bubbies, so round and so white;
By the Mole on your Neck, where my Arms would delight;
By whatever Mole else you have got out of Sight,
I prithee now hear me, dear Molly.

By the Kiss just a-starting from off your moist Lips;
By the delicate up-and-down Jutt of your Hips;
By the Tip of your Tongue, which all Tongues far out-tips;
I prithee, &c.

By the Down on your Bosom, on which my Soul dies;
By the Thing of all Things, which you love as your Eyes;
By the Thoughts you lie down with, and those when you
    rise,
I prithee, &c.

By all the soft Pleasure a Virgin can share;
By the critical Minute no Virgin can bear;
By the Question I burn so to ask, but don't dare,
I prithee now hear me, dear Molly.

SONG VIII.

When first I sought fair *Celia's* Love,
And every Charm was new,
I swore by all the Gods above
To be for ever true.

But long in vain did I adore,
Long wept and sigh'd in vain;
She still protested, vow'd and swore,
She ne'er would ease my Pain.

At last o'ercome, she made me blest,
And yielded all her Charms;
And I forsook her when possesst,
And fled to others' Arms.

But let not this, dear *Celia*, now
Thy Breast to Rage incline;
For why, since you forgot your Vow,
Shou'd I remember mine?

SONG IX.

No more, severely kind, affect
To put that lovely Anger on;
Sweet Tyrant! if thou can'st suspect
Thy Lover's Eyes, yet trust thy own.

Aw'd by stern Honour, watchful Spies,
Dull, formal Rules I'm forc'd t' obey;
Like Dungeon Slaves, my hasty Eyes
Just snatch a Glimpse of chearful Day.

Absent, the Desart Walks I view,
Here went *Eliza*, there she came;
With Tears my lonely Couch bedew,
And dreaming, sigh *Eliza's* Name.

"Where is his Soul?" the Women cry,
"The stupid Lump! the lifeless Earth;"
"Where," say the Men, "his brisk Reply,
"His crimson Glass, and noisy Mirth?"

Hast thou not mark'd my burning Kiss,
My lawless Pulse, my bounding Heart;
How oft, when wild for further Bliss,
All trembling from thy Arms I start?

Ah, spotless Fair, tho' well I find
My Passion's strong, my Reason's frail:
Ah, can I stain that Angel Mind,
And, Virtue lost, let Love prevail?

No! down in Shades below we'll rove,
A glorious miserable Pair;
Gaz'd at through all the Myrtle Grove,
For burning Love and chaste Despair.

Say, if thou lov'st, did ever Youth,
That wish'd like me, like me endure?
Do'st thou not blame this Swainish Truth,
And wish my Flame was not so pure?

In pity hate me, tempting Fair,
An happy Exile let me fly;
What fev'rish Wretch his Thirst can bear,
That sees the cooling Stream so nigh!

Oh! I shall all my Vows unsay,
If once I gaze—— my Blood will glow;
This virtuos Frost will melt away,
And Love's wild Torrent over-flow.

SONG X.

Phillis, we not grieve that Nature
Forming you has done her Part,
And in every single Feature
Shew'd the utmost of her Art.

But in this it is pretended
That a mighty Grievance lies;
That your Heart should be defended,
Whilst you wound us with your Eyes.

Love's a senseless Inclination,
When no Mercy's to be found;
But just, when kind Compassion
Gives us Balm to heal the Wound.

Persians paying solemn Duty
To the rising Sun inclined,
Never would adore his Beauty,
But in Hopes to make him kind.

SONG XI.

Tell me, *Cloe*, why has Nature
Been so partial to your Form;
Why in Beauty deck'd each Feature?
Think you 'twas to aid your Scorn?

No, mistaken charming Woman,
Nature no such Thrift requires;
She bestows her Gifts in common,
And our lib'ral Use desires.

Then no longer doat on Pow'r,
But let Love your Thoughts employ;
Use the now propitious Hour,
And improve the instant Joy.

Time, tho' slowly, is approaching
When that Face we now adore,
'Stead of Love will cause our Loathing,
Spread with Age and Wrinkles o'er.

Then when weakly, vainly prating,
You your former Conquests boast,
Who'll regard you, while relating
What your Scorn and Folly lost?

SONG XII.

Will you ever, lovely Charmer,
Still persist to tyranize?
Still, &c. ;
Can no Fire approach to warm her
Who from Danger never flies?
Who, &c.

Circled in a Crowd of Lovers,
Kindly all you entertain,
Kindly, &c. ;
None your favourite Smile discovers,
Yet we're pleas'd to live in Pain,
Yet, &c.

Yet believe me, lovely Creature,
Heaven design'd you kind as fair,
Heaven, &c. ;
Trust for once the God of Nature,
None are happy but a Pair,
None, &c.

SONG XIII.

O fly from this Place, dear *Flora*,
Thy Gaoler **has** set thee free;
And before the next Blush of *Aurora*,
You'll find a kind Guardian in me.

Dearest Creature, exchange for a better,
Confinement can have no Charms;
Think which of your Prisons is sweeter,
This or a young Lover's Arms.

SONG XIV.

Caelia, hoard thy Charms no more;
Beauty's like the Miser's Treasure;
Still the vain Possessor's poor;
What are Riches without Pleasure?

Endless Pain the Miser takes
To encrease his Heap of Money;
Lab'ring Bees his Pattern makes,
Yet he fears to taste his Honey.

Views with aking Eyes his Store,
Trembling, lest he chance to lose it;
Pining still for want of more,
Tho' the Wretch wants Pow'r to use it.

Caelia thus, with endless Arts,
Spends her Days her Charms improving;
Lab'ring still to conquer Hearts,
Yet ne'er tastes the Sweets of loving.

Views with Pride her Shape, her Face,
Fancying still she's under Twenty;
Age brings Wrinkles on apace,
While she starves with all her Plenty.

Soon or late they both will find
Time their Idol from them sever;
He must leave his Gold behind,
Lock'd within his Grave for ever.

Caelia's Fate will still be worse,
When her fading Charms deceive her;
Vain Desire will be her Curse,
When no Mortal will relieve her.

Caelia, hoard thy Charms no more;
Beauty's like the Miser's Treasure:
Taste a little of thy Store;
What is Beauty without Pleasure?

SONG XV.

Oh! my Treasure,
Crown my Pleasure;
Let this be the happy Night:
Bless, oh bless me!
Kindly press me,
Let me die with dear Delight.

Leave this Trembling
And Dissembling,
Lay aside all Female Art;
Love's soft Pleasure
Beyond Measure
Will atone for all its Smart.

SONG XVI.

Why shou'd coy Beauty be so hard
To be to Joy persuaded?
Why so perversely stand its guard,
By Love and Youth invaded?

Did ever Dame against the Knight,
Who came to her redressing,
For the rude Giant-Jailer fight,
And help her own oppressing?

Such Honour is, the tender Maid
With rigid Force restraining;
Love soon, with Leave, wou'd lend his Aid,
And end the Tyrant's reigning.

But, the poor **Fool's** so taught **to dread**
Her Friend, **her Foe** to favour,
She thinks it Ruin to be freed,
Protection **to enslave her.**

Be wise, ye Fair, and keep not dead
Upon your Hands your Treasure;
The honest Lover does but plead
For a fair Truck of Pleasure.

Between the Nymph and Swain that join
In Love, 'tis equal Trading;
He gains the Riches of her Mine,
And she his Vessel's Lading.

SONG XVII.

Amelia, art thou Mad,
To let the World, in me,
Envy Joys I never had,
And censure them in thee?

Fill'd with Grief for what is past,
Let us at length be wise,
And the Banquet boldly taste,
Since we have paid the Price.

Love does easy Souls despise,
Who lose themselves for Toys;
An Escape for those devise
Who taste his utmost Joys.

To be thus for Trifles blam'd
Like their's a Folly is,
Who are for vain Swearing damn'd,
And know no higher Bliss.

Love shou'd, like the Year, be crown'd
With sweet Variety;
Hope shou'd in Spring abound,
Kind Fears, and Jealousy.

In the Summer Flowers shou'd rise,
And in the Autumn Fruit;
His Spring doth else but mock our Eyes,
And in a Scoff salute.

SONG XVIII.

I love thee, by Heav'n; I cannot say more;
Then set not my Passion a-cooling:
If thou yield'st not at once I must e'en give thee o'er,
For I'm but a Novice at Fooling.

What my Love wants in Words it shall make up in Deeds;
Then why should we waste Time in Stuff, Child?
A Performance, you wot well, a Promise exceeds,
And a Word to the Wise is enough, Child.

I know how to love, and to make that Love known,
But I hate all protesting and argueing;
Had a Goddess my Heart, she shou'd e'en lie alone
If she made many Words to a Bargain.

I'm a Quaker in Love, and but barely affirm
Whate'er my fond Eyes have been saying;
Pr'ythee be thou so too, seek for no better Term,
But e'en throw thy Yea or thy Nay in.

I cannot bear Love, like a *Chancery* Suit,
The Age of a Patriarch depending;
Then pluck up a Spirit, no longer be mute,
Give it one Way or other an ending.

Long Courtship's the Vice of a phlegmatick Fool;
Like the Grace of fanatical Sinners,
When the Stomachs are lost, and the Victuals grow cool,
Before Men sit down to their Dinners.

SONG XIX.

Dear *Aminda*, in vain you so cooly refuse
What Nature and Love do inspire;
That formal old Way, which your Mother did use,
    Can never confine the desire;
    It rather adds Oil to the Fire.

When the tempting Delights of Wooing are lost,
And Pleasure a Duty becomes,
We both shall appear, like some dead Lover's Ghost,
    To frighten each other from Home;
    And the genial Bed like a Tomb.

Now low at your Feet your fond Lover will lie,
And seek a new Fate in your Eyes;
One amorous Smile will exalt him so high,
    He can all but *Aminda* despise;
    Then change to a Frown, and he dies.

To Love, and each other, we'll ever be true;
But to raise our Enjoyments by Art,
We'll often fall out, and as often renew;
    For to wound and cure the Smart
    Is the Pleasure which captures the Heart.

SONG XX.

Hence, hence, thou vain fantastic Fear
Of Ill to come, we know not where;
Stand not with thy infernal Face
To fright my Love from my Embrace;
To what a Height should we love on
Wert thou and all thy Shadows gone?

Sigh, sigh no more, nor cry; forbear,
'Tis Sin, I nuyther must nor dare;
If Sin can in these Pleasures dwell,
If this can be the Gate of Hell,
No Flesh can hold from ent'ring in;
Heav'n must forgive so sweet a Sin.

Down, down she does begin to fall,
And now the Shadows vanish all;
And now the Gate is ope to Bliss,
And now I'm entered Paradise;
Whilst envying Angels flock to view,
And wonder what it is we do.

SONG XXI.

Say, lovely *Sylvia*, leud and fair,
Venus in Face and Mind,
Why must not I that Bounty share
You pour on all Mankind?

That Sun that shines promiscuosly
On Prince and Porter's Head,
Why must it now leave only me
To languish in the Shade?

In vain you cry, You'll sin no more,
In vain you pray and fast;
You'll ne'er persuade us, till threescore,
That *Sylvia* can be chaste.

When thus affectedly you cant,
You're such a young Beginner,
You make at best an awkward Saint,
That are a charming Sinner.

SONG XXII.

There was a Swain full fair
Was tripping it over the Grass,
And there he spy'd with her nut-brown Hair
A pretty, tight Country Lass:
Fair Damsell, says he
With an Air brisk and free,
Come, let us each other know:
She blush'd in his Face,
And reply'd with a Grace,
Pray forbear, Sir; no, no, no, no, &c.

The Lad being bolder grown,
Endeavour'd to steal a Kiss;
She cry'd, Pish—let me alone,
But held up her Nose for the Bliss:
And when he begun
She would never have done,
But into his Lips she did grow;
Near smothered to Death,
As soon as she had Breath,
She stammer'd out, No, no, no, no, &c.

Come, come, says he, pretty Maid,
Let's to your private Grove;
Cupid always delights in the cooling Shade,
There I'll read thee a Lesson of Love:
She mends her Pace,
And hastens to the Place;
But if her Lecture you'd know,
Let a bashful young Muse
Plead the Maiden's Excuse,
And answer you, No, no, no, no, &c.

SONG XXIII.

By the Toast of your Health, when full Bumpers go down;
By the am'rous Masquerade Beaus of the Town;
By the powder'd pert Fop, and the rustic dull Clown,
I prithee now hear me, dear Cloe.

By the Pink of the Mode, which the Fair so adore;
By the Pride of the Sex, when their Smiles we implore;
By the Charms of your Dress, and the Force of its Pow'r,
I prithee, &c.

By the Posy display'd on your Ring, or your Garter;
By your delicate Snuff-box, enamell'd much smarter;
By the *Je-ne-scay-quoy*, when your Captives cry Quarter,
I prithee, &c.

By the simpering Dimple your Smiling discovers;
By the ogling Glance when you captivate Lovers;
By the coquetting Belles, who censure all others,
I prithee, &c.

By that Circle, your Hoop, which such Charms does inclose;
By your killing bright Eyes, and your aquiline Nose;
By the Death they commit, when a Spark you depose,
I prithee, &c.

By your Lips so ambrosial, and Bosom so fair;
By your Parrot's fine Prattle, which charms your fine Ear;
By the gen'rous young Sylphs who make you their Care,
I prithee, &c.

By your Lilly-white Hands, and Fingers so pretty;
By your exquisite Genius, facetious and witty;
By all the gay Fancies described in this Ditty,
I prithee now hear me, dear Cloe.

SONG XXIV.

Why should a Heart so tender break?
O *Myra!* give its Anguish Ease;
The Use of Beauty you mistake,
Nor meant to vex, but please.

Those Lips for Smiling were design'd,
That Bosom to be prest,
Your Eyes to languish and look kind,
For amorous Arms your Waste.

Each Thing has its appointed Right,
Establish'd by the Powers above;
The Sun and Stars give Warmth and Light,
The Fair distribute Love.

SONG XXV.

Come, dearest *Flavia*, pray be kind;
Why should you shun, why longer slight me?
You'll find in Love all Pleasures join'd,
And share the Joys whilst you delight me.

Why should you be averse to Bliss,
Whilst I in boundless Transports die?
You'll feel the rapt'rous Extasies,
And cease to breathe as well as I.

Let us the happy Time improve,
Now Time and Place do both conspire;
Time swiftly flies away in Love,
Then let us gratify Desire.

(She yields, I see it in her Eyes.)
You'll find true Bliss in Love alone;
How vast must be the rapt'rous Joys
Where every Sense is bless'd in one.

THE HAPPY LOVER.

SONG I.

The Lass of *Peaty's* Mill,
So bonny, blith, and gay,
In spite of all my Skill,
Hath stole my Heart away:
When tedding of the Hay
Bare-headed on the Green,
Love midst her Locks did play,
And wanton in her Een.

Her Arms white, round, and smooth,
Breasts rising in their Dawn;
To Age it would give Youth
To press them with his Hand:
Thro' all my Spirits ran
An Extacy of Bliss,
When I such Sweetness found
Wrapt in a balmy Kiss.

SONG II.

Ye watchful Guardians of the Fair,
Who skiff on Wings of ambient Air,
Let my dear *Delia* be your Care,
And represent her Lover,
With all the Gaity of Youth,
With Honour, Justice, Love, and Truth;
Till I return her Passion sooth,
For me in Whispers move her.

Be careful no base sordid Slave,
With Soul sunk in a sordid Grave,
Who knows no Virtue but to save,
With glaring Gold bewitch her:

Tell her for me she was designed,
For me, who knows how to be kind,
And have more Plenty in my Mind
Than one that's ten times richer.

SONG III.

Poor *Damon* knocked at *Caelia's* Door,
He sigh'd and begged, and wept and swore;
    The Sign was so:
    She answered, No,
    No, no, no; *Damon*, no.

Again he sigh'd, again he pray'd;
No, *Damon*, no, I am afraid;
Consider, *Damon*, I'm a Maid,
    Consider; no,
    I am a Maid,
    No, &c.

At last his Sighs and Tears made Way;
She rose, and softly turned the Key:
Come in, said she, but do not stay;
    I may conclude
    You will be rude,
But if you will you may.

SONG IV.

Is *Hamilla* then my own?
O! the dear, the charming Treasure!
Fortune now in vain shall frown,
All my future Life is Pleasure.

See how rich with Youthful Grace,
Beauty warms her every Feature;
Smiling Heaven is in her Face,
All is gay, and all is Nature.

See what mingling Charms arise,
Rosy Smiles and kindling Blushes;
Love sits laughing in her Eyes,
And betrays her secret Wishes.

Haste then from the Idalian Grove,
Infant Smiles, and Sports and Graces,
Spread the downy Couch for Love,
And lull us in your sweet Embraces.

Softest Raptures, pure from Noise,
This fair happy Night surround us;
While a thousand spritely Joys
Silent flutter all around us.

Thus unsour'd with Care or **Strife**,
Heaven still guard this dearest Blessing;
While we tread the Path of Life,
Loving still, and still possessing.

SONG V.

Transported with Pleasure,
I gaze on my Treasure,
And ravish my Sight,
And **ravish** my Sight;
While **she** gaily smiling,
My Anguish beguiling,
Augments my Delight.

How blest **is a Lover**
Whose Torments are over,
His Fears **and** his Pain,
His Fears and his Pain;
When Beauty, relenting,
Repays with consenting
Her Scorn and Disdain.

SONG VI.

May the Ambitious ever find
Success in Crowds and Noise,
While gentle Love does fill my Mind
With silent real Joys.

May Knaves and Fools grow rich and great,
And all the World think them Wise,
While I lie at my *Nanny's* Feet,
And all the World despise.

Let conquering Kings new Conquests raise,
And melt in Court Delights;
Her Eyes can give much brighter Days,
Her Arms much softer Nights.

SONG VII.

Behold I fly on Wings of soft Desire,
Whilst gentle Zephyrs waft me on;
Eager as when a Bridegroom, all on Fire,
Longs from the Company to be gone:
    She blushing flies the Pleasure,
    He rushing grasps his Treasure,
Till with mutual Tenderness each other they warm:
    Since *Phaebe's* my Guide,
    And Love does preside,
    Each Monarch, tho' great,
    Wou'd envy my State,
For she, she alone has the Power to charm.

SONG VIII.

When I survey *Clarinda's* Charms,
Folded within my circling Arms,
What endless Pleasures move along,
Serenely soft, and sweetly strong;
Every Smile invites to Love;
    Balmy Kisses,
    Am'rous Blisses,
Every rising Charm improve.

Love on her Breast has fixt his Throne,
And *Cupid* revels in her Eyes;
Who can the Charmer's Power disown,
When in each Glance an Arrow flies?
Yet when wounded we feel no Pain;
    No, 'tis Pleasure
    Above Measure;
Raptures flow in every Vein.

SONG IX.

No, *Delia*, no; what Man can range
From such Seraphick Pleasure?
'Tis want of Charms that make us change,
To grasp the Fairy Treasure:
What Man of Sense wou'd quit a certain Bliss
For Hopes, and empty Possibilities?

Vain Fools **their sure** Possessions spend
In Hopes of Chymic Treasure,
But for their fancy'd Riches find
Both want of Gold and Pleasure:
Rich in my *Delia*, I can wish no more;
The Wanderer, like the Chymist, must be poor.

SONG X.

As *Caelia* near a Fountain lay,
Her Eye-lids closed with Sleep,
The Shepherd *Damon* chanc'd that Way
To drive his Flock of Sheep,
To drive, &c.

With awful Steps he approach'd **the Fair**,
To view her charming Face,
Where every Feature wore an Air,
And every Part a Grace,
And every, &c.

His Heart inflamed with am'rous Pain,
He wished the Nymph would wake,
Tho' ne'er before was any Swain
So unprepared to speak,
So unprepared, &c.

Whilst slumbering thus fair *Caelia* lay,
Soft Wishes filled her Mind;
She cried, Come, *Thyrsis*, come away,
For now I will be kind,
For now, &c.

Damon embraced the lucky Hit,
And flew into her Arms;
He took her in the yielding Fit,
And rifled all her Charms,
And rifled, &c.

SONG XI.

Cloe, when I view thee smiling,
Joys coelestial round me move;
Pleasing Visions Care beguiling,
Guard my State and crown my Love:

To behold thee gaily shining
Is a Pleasure past defining;
Every Feature charms my Sight:
But, oh Heav'ns! when I'm caressing,
Thrilling Raptures never ceasing,
Fill my Soul with soft Delight.

O! thou lovely dearest **Creature**,
Sweet Enslaver of my **Heart**!
Beauteous Master-piece **of Nature**,
Cause of all my Joy and Smart!
In thy Arms enfolded lay me,
To dissolving Bliss convey me,
Softly sooth my Soul to rest;
Gently, kindly, oh my Treasure!
Bless me, let me die with Pleasure
On thy panting snowy Breast.

SONG XII.

Whilst *Alexis* lay prest
In her Arms he loved best,
With his Hand round her Neck,
And his Head on her Breast,
He found the fierce Pleasure too hasty to stay,
And his Soul in the Tempest fast flying away.

When *Caelia* saw this,
With a Sigh and a Kiss
She cried, Oh my Dear, I am robbed of my Bliss;
'Tis unkind to your Love, and unfaithfully done,
To leave me behind you, and die all alone.

The Youth, tho' in Haste,
And breathing his last,
In Pity dy'd slowly, while she dy'd more fast;
Till at length she cry'd—Now, my Dear, now let us go;
Now die, my *Alexis*, and I will die too.

Thus intranced they did lie,
Till *Alexis* did try
To recover new Breath, that again he might die;
Then often they dy'd; but the more they did so,
The Nymph dy'd more quick, and the Shepherd more slow.

K

SONG XIII.

Upon *Clarinda's* panting Breast
The happy *Strephon* lay,
With Love and Beauty jointly prest
To pass the Time away;
Fresh Raptures of transporting **Love**
Have struck his Senses dumb;
He envies not the Power above,
Nor all the Joys to come.

As painful Bees abroad do rove
To fetch their Treasures home,
So *Strephon* rov'd the Fields of Love
To fill her Honey-comb;
Her ruby Lips he kist and prest,
From whence all Joys derive;
Then humming round her snowy Breast,
Straight crept into **her Hive.**

SONG XIV.

When *Cloe* shines serenely gay,
Oh! how Love's Goddess she outvies!
How on her Lips the Graces play,
And *Cupids* wanton in her Eyes!

What soft Delights her Smiles impart!
What Raptures does young *Damon* **feel,**
When thus she ravishes his Heart
With Joys **too mighty to reveal!**

Let the Conceited of her Sex
Requite, with Scorn, the Lover's Pain;
Let them take Pleasure to perplex,
And triumph o'er a dying Swain.

The Nymph must have a heavenly Mind,
A Soul that's gen'rous, **great,** and brave;
Who conquers only to **be kind,**
And makes it her Delight to **save.**

The God-like *Romans* so (tho' crown'd,
Where-e'er they came, with Victory)
Not for their Arms were more renown'd
Than for their Acts of Clemency.

SONG XV.

As *Damon* late with *Cloe* sat,
They talked of Am'rous Blisses;
Kind Things he said, which she repaid
In pleasing Smiles and Kisses:
With tuneful Tongue, of Love he sung;
She thank'd him for his Ditty;
But said, One Day she heard him say,
The Flute was mighty pretty.

Young *Damon*, who her meaning knew,
Took out his Pipe to charm her;
And while he strove, with wanton Love,
And sprightly Airs to warm her,
She begged the Swain to play one Strain,
In all the softest Measure,
Whose killing Sound would sweetly wound,
And make her die with Pleasure.

Eager to do't, he takes the Flute,
And every Accent traces;
Love tickling through his Fingers flew,
And whispered Melting Graces:
He played his Part with wondrous Art,
Expecting Praises after;
But she, instead of falling dead,
Burst out into a Laughter.

Taking the Hint, as *Cloe* meant,
Said he, My Dear be easy;
I have a Flute, which tho' 'tis mute.
May play a Tune to please ye:
Then down he laid the charming Maid;
He found her kind and willing:
He played again, and tho' each Strain
Was silent, yet 'twas killing.

Fair *Cloe* soon approved the Tune,
And vow'd he play'd divinely;
Let's have it o'er, said she, once more,
It goes exceeding finely:
The Flute is good that's made of Wood,
And is, I own, the neatest;
Yet ne'ertheless, I must confess,
The Silent Flute's the sweetest.

SONG XVI.

Hail to the Myrtile Shade,
All hail to the Nymphs of the Fields;
Kings wou'd not here invade
Those Pleasures that Virtue yields.
CHORUS.
Beauty here opens her Arms
To soften the languishing Mind;
And Phillis *unlocks her Charms;*
Ah Phillis*! ah, why so kind?*

Phillis, thou Soul of Love,
Thou Joy of the neighbouring Swains;
Phillis that crowns the Grove,
And *Phillis* that gilds the Plains.
CHORUS.
Phillis *that ne'er had the Skill*
To paint, to patch, and be fine;
Yet Phillis *whose Eyes can kill,*
Whom Nature hath made divine.

Phillis, whose charming Song
Makes Labour and Pains a Delight;
Phillis, that makes Day young,
And shortens the live-long Night.
CHORUS.
Phillis, *whose Lips like May*
Still laughs at the Sweets that they bring;
Where Love never knows Decay,
But sets with eternal Spring.

SONG XVII.

As I beneath the Myrtle Shade lay musing,
Sylvia the fair, in mournful Sounds
Venting her Grief, the Air thus wounds:
Oh! God of Love, cease to torment me;
Send to my Aid some gentle Swain,
Whose Balm apply'd may ease my Pain.

Aloud I cry'd, and all the Grove resounded,
Heavenly Nymph, complain no more;
Love does thy wish'd for Peace restore,
And send a gentle Swain to ease thee,
In whom a longing Maid may find
A Balm to cure her Love-sick Mind.

She blush'd, and sigh'd, and pushed the Med'cine from her,
Which still the more encreased her Pain:
Finding at length she strove in vain,
Oh! Love, she cry'd, I must obey thee;
Who can the raging Smart endure?
Then sucked the Balm and found a Cure.

SONG XVIII.

As *Chloris*, full of harmless Thought,
Beneath a Myrtle lay,
Kind Love a youthful Shepherd brought,
To pass the Time away.

She blushed to be encounter'd so,
And chid the am'rous Swain;
But as she strove to rise, and go,
He pulled her down again.

A sudden Passion seized **her Heart**
In spite of her Disdain;
She found a Pulse in every Part,
And Love in every Vein.

Ah! Gods! said she, what Charms are these,
That conquer and surprize?
Oh! let me—for unless you please,
I have no Power to rise.

She fainting spoke and trembling lay,
For fear he should comply;
Her Looks and Eyes her Heart betray,
And gave her Tongue the Lye.

Thus she, who Princes had deny'd,
With all their Pomp and Train,
Was in the lucky Minute try'd,
And yielded to a Swain.

SONG XIX.

Whilst on *Melanissa* gazing,
I survey each pleasing Grace,
And, with eager Joys embracing,
Dwell on that Angelick Face.

There, with endless Raptures kissing,
I could breathe my Soul away;
But my Eyes, the Pleasure missing,
Chide my Lip's too long Delay.

Lest the Eye shou'd want its Longing,
I a while quit t'other Bliss;
But my Lips, their Loss bemoaning,
Prompt me to another Kiss.

Thus perpetually renewing
Those two never-fading Joys,
Kissing her, by turns, and viewing,
Pleas'd I feast both Lips and Eyes.

SONG XX.

Phillis has a gentle Heart,
Willing to her Lover's Courting
Wanton Nature, all Love's Art,
To direct her in her Sporting:
In th' Embrace, the Look, the Kiss,
All is real Inclination;
No false Raptures in the Bliss,
No feign'd Sighings in the Passion.

But O, who the Charms can speak,
Who the thousand Ways of toying,
When she does the Lover make
All a God in the enjoying?
Who the Limbs that round him move,
And constrain him to her Blisses?
Who the Eyes that swim in Love,
Or the Lips that suck in Kisses?

O the Freaks when mad she grows,
Raves all wild with the Possessing!
O the silent Trance that shows
The Delight above expressing!
Every Way she does engage,
Idly talking, speechless lying;
She transports me with her Rage,
And she kills me in her Dying.

SONG XXI.

I gently touch'd her Hand, she gave
A Look that did my Soul enslave;

I prest her Rebel-Lips, in vain;
They rose up to be prest again:
Thus happy, I no further meant
Than to be pleased and innocent.

On her soft Breasts my Hand I laid,
And a quick light Impression made;
They with a kindly Warmth did glow,
And swell'd and seem'd to over-flow;
Yet, trust me, I no further meant
Than to be pleased and innocent.

On her Eyes my Eyes did stay,
O'er her smooth Limbs my Hand did stray;
Each Sense was ravished with Delight,
And my Soul stood prepared for Flight;
Blame not me if, at last, I meant
More to be pleased than innocent.

SONG XXII.

An am'rous Swain to *Juno* pray'd,
And thus his Suit did move,
Give me, oh! give me the dear Maid,
Or take away my Love.

The Goddess thunder'd from the Skies,
And granted his Request;
To make him happy, made him wise,
And drove her from his Breast.

SONG XXIII.

Say, mighty Love, and teach my Song,
To whom thy sweetest Joys belong,
And who the happy Pairs,
Whose yielding Hearts and joining Hands
Find Blessings twisted with their Bands,
To soften all their Cares.

Not the wild Herd of Nymphs and Swains,
That thoughtless fly into the Chains,
As Custom leads the Way:
If there be Bliss without Design,
Ivies and Oaks may grow and twine,
And be as blest as they.

Not sordid Souls of earthly Mould,
Who, drawn by kindred Charms of Gold,
To dull Embraces move:
So two rich Mountains of *Peru*
May rush to wealthy Marriage too,
And make a World of Love.

Nor the mad Tribe that Hell inspires
With wanton Flames, those raging Fires—
The purer Bliss destroy:
On *Etna's* Top let Furies wed,
And Sheets of Lightning dress the Bed,
T' improve the burning Joy.

Nor the dull Pairs whose Marble Forms
None of the melting Passions warms,
Can mingle Hearts and Hands;
Logs of green Wood that quench the Coals
Are married just like *Stoick* Souls,
With offers for their Bands.

Not Minds of melancholy Strain,
Still silent, or that still complain,
Can the dear Bondage bless:
As well may heavenly Consorts spring
From two old Lutes with ne'er a String,
Or none beside the Bass.

Nor can the soft Enchantments hold
Two jarring Souls of angry Mould,
The rugged and the keen:
Sampson's young Foxes might as well
In Bonds of chearful Wedlock dwell,
With Fire-brands ty'd between.

Nor let the cruel Fetters bind
A gentle to a savage Mind,
For Love abhors the Sight:
Loose the fierce Tyger from the Deer,
For native Rage and native Fear
Rise and forbid Delight.

Two kindest Souls alone must meet;
'Tis Friendship makes the Bondage sweet,
And feeds their mutual Loves;
Bright *Venus* on her rolling Throne
Is drawn by gentlest Birds alone,
And *Cupids* yoke the Doves.

SONG XXIV.

As *Damon* watch'd his harmless Sheep
Within a silent Shade,
Lock'd in the Bands of downy Sleep,
He saw his Charmer laid;
And thus he hail'd the beauteous Maid:
AIR.
Close not those charming Eyes,
My Life, my only Dear!
'Tis Night they arise,
'Tis Day when they appear.

Charm'd with the tuneful Accents of his Voice,
The lovly Virgin rear'd her Head;
For *Damon's* Song makes Sorrow's Self rejoice,
So sweet! 'twould e'en recal the Dead:
Nor was the Nymph coquet or coy,
Too well she knew the artless Boy;
With Fervour, not to be exprest,
She clasped him to her snowy Breast,
Who thus sang forth his Joy:
AIR.
While in her Arms my Charmer holds me,
I think the Queen of Love infolds me;
Less lovely *Venus* is than she,
Adonis far less blest than me.

SONG XXV.

Musing on Cares of human Fate,
In a sad Cypress Grove,
A strange Dispute I heard of late,
'Twixt *Virtue, Fame,* and *Love:*
A pensive Shepherd ask'd Advice,
And their Opinions crav'd,
How he might hope to be so wise
To get a Place beyond the Skies,
And how he might be sav'd.

Nice *Virtue* preach'd Religion's Laws,
Paths to eternal Rest;
To fight his King's and Country's Cause
Fame councell'd him was best;

But *Love* oppos'd their noisy Tongues,
And thus their Votes out-brav'd:
Get, get a Misstress, fair and young,
Love fiercely, constantly, and long,
And then thou shalt be sav'd.

Swift as a Thought the am'rous Swain
To *Sy'via's* Cottage flies;
In soft Expressions told her plain
The Way to heav'nly Joys:
She, who with Pity was stor'd,
Delays no longer crav'd;
Charm'd by the God whom they ador'd,
She smil'd and took him at his Word;
And thus they both were sav'd.

SONG XXVI.

As on a vernal Evening fair,
Damon and *Celia* (happy Pair!)
Sate on a flow'ry Bank reclin'd,
Beneath a fragrant Myrtle Shade,
While their young Offspring round 'em play'd,
Thus ravish'd *Damon* op'd his Mind:

Oh! what happy State is this!
My *Celia!* what a Heav'n of Bliss
Does Love, pure, lawful Love supply!
Whether I turn my Look on thee,
Or yonder Infant Charmer see,
Still Views of Joy salute my Eye.

Life's highest Blessings all are mine,
And doubly so by being thine,
Dear Crown of all that I enjoy!
No anxious guilty Thoughts I find
To discompose my Peace of Mind,
Pure Love yields Sweets without Alloy.

I draw no ruin'd Virgin's Tear,
No injured Parent's Curse I hear;
I dread no violated Laws;
I lose no Honour, waste no Wealth;
With no Diseases wound my Health,
Foul as the shameful Crime their Cause.

Our holy Union Heav'n approves,
And smiles indulgent on our Loves,
As our unnumber'd Blessings show:
Oh! let our Virtue then improve,
Let us secure more Bliss above;
For more we cannot wish below.

FINIS.

DERBY, LEICESTER, AND NOTTINGHAM: FRANK MURRAY.

www.ingramcontent.com/pod-product-compliance
Lightning Source LLC
Chambersburg PA
CBHW032229230426
43666CB00033B/1646